Acknowledgments

This book, inspired by God, has been created with the help of many people. I would like to acknowledge and thank:

Laurie Masters and Colleen Holland, copy editors
Jeannie Collins, consultant and illustrator
Lynn Piquett, cover designer
Tony Grant, cover photographer
Paul Schraub, portrait photographer
Creative X-Pressions, graphic design and typesetting

Keith and Kerrie Adams, for being the loves of my life

Claudia Aebersold, for her love and support

Gayle Bradshaw, for introducing me to Pam Masters and being a great friend

Tom Calabro, my wonderful brother

Jason Cronin, for his love, support, and for helping me get well

Richard Salome, for his words of wisdom

Janis Weiss, for encouraging me to become a vegetarian

Friends who contributed recipes

Dedication

This book
is dedicated to Pam Masters,
who taught me about living food
and how to heal my body. Because
of her love, support and devotion to
living food, Pam was a major
contributor to saving my life.
Pam will always hold a
special place in
my heart.

Living in the Raw

Recipes for a Healthy Lifestyle

Rose Lee Calabro

Rose Publishing, Santa Cruz, California

Living in the Raw
Recipes for a Healthy Lifestyle
by Rose Lee Calabro

Published by: **Rose Publishing**
P.O. Box 2274
Santa Cruz, CA 95063
(831) 768-7400   (877) 557-4711
e-mail: rose@rawlivingfoods.com
website: www. rawlivingfoods.com

Publisher's Cataloging-in-Publication (Provided by Quality Books, Inc.)
Calabro, Rose Lee
        Living in the raw : recipes for a healthy lifestyle / Rose Lee
        Calabro.
        p. cm.
        Includes index.
        ISBN: 0-9666816-0-6
        1. Vegetarian cookery.   I. Title.

        TX837.C35 1999   641.5'636
                                QBI98-1117

Printed in the United States of America
10 9 8 7 6 5 4 3 2

My purpose for this book is to help people create a new lifestyle and transition to raw living foods.

Foreword

Living in the Raw is one of the best living food recipe books I have read. It provides an excellent introduction, not only to living foods, but also to the living foods lifestyle. The lessons Rose Lee Calabro learned from her own transition to living foods, including the internal psychospiritual and external lifestyle changes associated with this transition to health, are still fresh for her. Rose Lee's freshness gives a delightful and insightful energy to *Living in the Raw.*

One of the most important principles in this book is freshness. The distinction Rose Lee makes between living foods and raw foods is insightful. Fresh foods are filled with biogenic energy that adds energy to our bodies in an amplified way. Once food is cut off from its life force source in the earth it begins to lose its energy. Raw food is still filled with more life-force energy than any cooked food. This principle of living food is why we serve our food fresh picked from our garden at the Tree of Life Rejuvenation Center each day and why it is so important to grow your own garden or at least have a sprout garden. Part of the usefulness of this book is that Rose Lee explains how to's of the transition skills such as growing a sprout garden and dehydrating.

Live foods connect us to life. This is a key point in Rose Lee's work. As a live food diet begins to deepen our connection to life, we open to the joy of the living planet and of all life around us. When we bite into living foods we are biting into the life force of the planet. We are taking in food as a love offering from the Divine in the way it was originally offered to us. The transition to living foods becomes a seduction into the joy of life.

As a holistic physician on living foods since 1983, I have had the opportunity to observe many people open to life and to spirit, as Rose Lee has in her transition to living foods and the living foods lifestyle.

One of the reasons I started the Tree of Life Rejuvenation Center in the mountains of Patagonia, Arizona is to help people accelerate and ground their transition to the living foods lifestyle. It amazes me that in the short time people stay with us, with the proper educational support and yoga and meditation experience people open quickly to the joy of the living foods lifestyle to which Rose Lee refers. Rose Lee herself had a new level of spiritual awakening while at the Tree of Life. It is wonderful to witness how living foods open us to the experience of the sacred in our lives. I consistently find that many of the spiritual processes are amplified with live foods: meditation, contemplation, flexibility in yoga, increased psychic abilities, and more experience of the Divine. Although, as I point out in *Spiritual Nutrition and The Rainbow Diet*, you can not eat your way to God, it sure makes walking the path a lot easier and quicker. Living foods accelerate the flow of cosmic energy in the body.

It has been my observation that although there are changes almost right away on living foods, it takes about two years for the deeper levels of optimal health to emerge. For example, as I point out in *Conscious Eating*, living foods even help us normalize at the optimal weight for longevity. This is because one only needs about half the calories, proteins, fats, and carbohydrates on a living food diet that they need on cooked food, because 50% of the protein and 70 – 90% of the vitamins and minerals are not destroyed through the cooking process. One is able to eat well on the amount of calories from a living food diet and come much closer to the low number of calories recommended for optimal longevity.

Contrary to what most people imagine, one can grow not only healthier, but also physically stronger, on living food. At the age of 21 as a captain of an undefeated college football team, I could do 70 push-ups; now, 35 years later I have done as many as 320 push-ups. With proper and intelligent intake of living food in a way that supports your constitution you only get better.

I appreciate the full range of recipes in *Living in the Raw*. They are listed in a way that acquaints one with the great culinary diversity available with living food. A live food cuisine can be cleansing or building, heating or cooling, good for winter or summer, or high or low in protein, depending on one's constitutional needs. This book gives recipes that apply for every season and for every constitution. In doing so it helps to break the stereotype that raw foods are only for cleansing.

Rose Lee Calabro has done a great job in creating a user-friendly living food inspiration, live food recipes and a lifestyle transition book. I will be carrying it at the Tree of Life bookstore. This book is an important guide to the simple, joyous way of living food.

Gabriel Cousens, MD (H)

Director of the Tree of Life Rejuvenation Center

Author of *Conscious Eating* and *Spiritual Nutrition and The Rainbow Diet*

About the Author

Over six years ago, I began a journey that would take me to places and achievements I never thought possible. It all started on July 1, 1992 when I went to see a nutritionist for a whole host of health issues including high cholesterol (239), high blood pressure (154/95), allergies, joint pain, depression, mood swings, gallstones, hair loss, hearing loss, hypoglycemia, hypothyroidism, difficulty concentrating, chronic sinusitis, insomnia, early signs of cancer in my breasts and lungs, and a severe case of gout.

I had endured these health issues for up to 20 years, but was never motivated to address them, due to low self-esteem because of being overweight since age seven. My motivation came from the passing of my father at age 59 due to lung cancer and the death of my mother due to heart failure at age 69. My mother also had high blood pressure, high cholesterol, diabetes and gout.

I began seeing a nutritionist every week to learn about vitamins, minerals, healthy food and the role they play in better health. I began eating a low-fat diet and entirely eliminated red meat from my diet. The first thing I noticed was that I began to lose weight, although that was not my original intention. As the weight came off, I began to feel better about myself and eventually made the commitment to lose all my excess weight. I made two promises to myself: 1.) I would never give up, and 2.) I would never regain the weight. I had been overweight my entire life,

Living in the Raw

and I didn't want to suffer the agony and low self-esteem of regaining the weight.

So for the next four years I searched to find the answer to the ongoing question in my life: how to eat and not gain weight. I first read all of Covert Bailey's books and attended one of his seminars in Sacramento. Covert Bailey and Rhonda Gates were a big inspiration in my life and furthered my knowledge on weight loss, exercise and nutrition. The first year I lost 60 pounds, my blood pressure dropped to normal, and my cholesterol dropped from 239 to 219. I struggled for the next couple of years gaining 20 pounds and losing 20 pounds. However, I never gave up and continued my search for answers.

In November 1994, I met Neal Barnard and read his book and began thinking about becoming a vegetarian. In February 1995, I attended a seminar with John and Mary McDougall. As a result of the seminar and influence from my dear friend Janis Weiss, I became a (cooked food) vegan. My health improved and cholesterol dropped to 198.

In February 1996, I became very sick and tired and was diagnosed with a high level of candida and chronic fatigue. I became so sick that it was a chore just getting out of a chair and difficult to concentrate on my work. My job was extremely stressful, and I realized my marriage was not bringing me the happiness and joy it once did. My doctor put me on disability, and I went home to heal.

I began reading every book I could find on candida. As a result of my reading, I discovered the benefits of colonics. I discussed it with my alternative medical doctor, and we agreed that I should pursue the treatment. He recommended Gayle Marie Bradshaw, a colon hydrotherapist. I had a total of twelve colonics, and with each session, I discovered new things about myself. Also, I uncovered experiences from my childhood that had caused me to overeat. With each colonic old feces, toxins and candida were eliminated, and I started to feel better.

In April 1996, Gayle told me about Pam Masters, who was going to give a living food class in Gayle's home. I attended Pam's introductory class and then signed up for an eight-week course. Within three weeks my diet consisted of 80% raw living foods. I was delighted to find myself once again losing weight (I had been at a plateau for two years). This time, the weight began to literally melt off my body — I was losing three, four and five pounds a week. I had finally found the answer to controlling my weight: raw living foods. And the longer I ate living food, the better I felt.

I began to change — mind, body and soul. Also, I learned about fasting, and how it would help to heal the body. I did five fasts within a year and a half. Wheatgrass is another staple of my diet and a great tool for healing the body. After six months of living food my chronic fatigue was gone, and I lost an additional 55 pounds for a total of 150 pounds of fat.

I have been on raw living food since April 1996, and my body has gone through some dramatic changes. My cholesterol has dropped to 151, and I no longer have the chronic fatigue, allergies, joint pain, depression, mood swings, gallstones, hair loss, hearing loss, hypoglycemia, hypothyroidism, difficulty concentrating, chronic sinusitis, insomnia, gout, and cancer.

Raw living foods has given me happiness, joy, a new life, and a new purpose for being on the planet. I have experienced a spiritual awakening and a closeness to God. I left a marriage of 23 years and got divorced. I moved to beautiful Santa Cruz to heal my body. I have a new career and do not plan to return to the corporate world. I have started Rose Publishing to publish and promote living foods books. My dream is to have a retreat facility in a farm setting and teach people how they can heal their body and have radiant health.

All my new friends are raw living food vegetarians, and they provide me with love, encouragement and a friendship that is everlasting. My life is filled with love, joy, and a happiness I have never experienced. My life is perfect!

Table of Contents

Table of Contents

What Are Living Foods?

The first questions that inevitably come up as I talk with people about incorporating more raw living foods into their diets are "What exactly are living foods?" and "Why are raw living foods better than processed foods?" These are excellent questions, both of which I had when I was first introduced to the idea that there was something called living foods.

As I quickly learned, the best answers to these questions come through experiencing living foods. There was no doubt in my mind after being on them for just one month that they were providing my body, my mind and my soul with something none of the other foods and diets I had ever tried gave me.

I now realize that living foods are the MVP (most valuable player) superstars of all foods. They are the Michael Jordans, Willie Mayses, and Joe Montanas of nutrition — raw foods in their most nutritious state. When living foods are added to any meal (especially one that's at least 50% raw), they add a new dimension to its nutritional value, namely an extraordinary ability to heal the body and the mind. They truly are like medicine without any side effects.

The easiest way to recognize a living food is to answer this question: "Is it still growing?" If yes, it's a living food. Good examples of living foods are vegetables and fruits growing wild or in your garden. My favorite memories of eating living foods are when I would pick wild berries and find myself eating most of them before I got home, or when I would be tempted to bite into a tomato that I had just picked out of my garden. I even remember once pretending I was Bugs Bunny and biting into a carrot right after pulling it from the ground and wiping it clean. "What's up, Doc?" It's an incredible experience I call "from garden to mouth." Those of you who have had similar experiences know what I mean when I say there is a distinct difference in the flavor and the energy that these foods provide.

For those of you not fortunate enough to have grown up around a garden, today in our supermarkets you can find new sources of living foods in the form of fresh sprouts and baby greens, which are alive and still growing as you "pick" them off the shelf. These are young living plants that can add valuable missing nutrition to your meals, especially your salads.

In this book, you will learn how to prepare a whole new world of tasty living foods right in your own kitchen. The techniques take minimum effort and result in fantastic health benefits.

Raw foods are the other stars of health and nutrition. Just remember this about raw foods: the older they get, the fewer nutrients they contain. Think about this: when any living food is picked, it is separated from its life energy source (its "umbilical connection" to Mother Earth), and its growth begins to slow. Within 24 to 48 hours after being picked, all growth stops. This is when a living food becomes an "adult" raw food. Now, as days go by, a raw food's powerful healing energies begin to slowly "radiate out." This may be evidenced by a change in color, a softer texture, a wrinkled appearance, a sweeter taste, etc. Be aware of this and choose only the freshest raw produce as you shop.

When there's an occasion that I find myself without raw living foods, every part of me misses them. This has happened at restaurants where menu choices were limited to mostly cooked items. Or at long seminars when only baked snacks and coffee were available during the short breaks. I notice now that within an hour after eating a meal that doesn't contain enough raw living foods, my body gets tired and even slightly achy, and my mind is not as clear as I've become accustomed to. My body and mind very quickly say, "Go find some raw living food, pleeeease." And it has taken up to two days after returning to my preferred meals to fully recover my "performing edge" as I call it.

And let me tell you — I love feeling at the top of my game.

I have learned that processed (i.e., cooked) foods have zero vital healing energies in them. It's instant death for the food when it's cooked. If you doubt this, try jumping into a pot of boiling water and see how long you last. Better yet, so that you can be alive to tell your story, try planting two types of seeds, raw and roasted (or boiled if you think they have a better chance to grow). I guarantee only one of these types will grow. That's life (and death), folks.

Nutritionally speaking, living foods are the richest sources of enzymes, oxygen, chlorophyll, vitamins, essential fatty acids, and fiber, and contain the proper ratio of alkaline to acid minerals. Raw foods follow a close second, with all our cooked and store-bought processed foods a very distant third.

Is this beginning to make some sense? Great. Let's do a quick review and see that we've answered the two questions that I opened this chapter with. First, a living food is one that is still growing. Great examples are fruits and vegetables that are eaten within two days of being picked, or the still-growing sprouts that you can find in your health food stores or supermarkets. In this book, you'll learn how you can expand the variety of living foods available to you and your family using techniques that I share with you.

Raw foods look very similar to living foods except that they are no longer growing. Most living foods become merely raw foods within 24 to 48 hours after they have been harvested (the exception are the sprouts you buy at the store). Slightly less nutritious, raw foods are still very beneficial to your health as long as they are still fresh. Along with living foods, they provide an incredible power to heal both the body and the mind. The great news is that raw foods can virtually be brought back to life using some of the preparation techniques that I share with you in this book.

Finally, there are the cooked or otherwise processed foods, which 95% of us eat 95% of the time. These foods have no healing powers whatsoever, which is perhaps why many doctors still do not feel that foods can heal. And I have not found a way to bring these cooked foods back to life. Though I don't focus on these types of food in this book, I mention them because the latest nutritional research clearly suggests that these foods contribute to many of our illnesses, chronic diseases, and premature deaths. So begin today to substitute raw living foods for cooked ones whenever possible.

This book is filled with raw living food recipes that will definitely increase your energy level and support you to become more of the superstar that you are meant to be. They will help you achieve your highest dreams and personal goals. In a relatively short period of time, you will find yourself thinking much more clearly with remarkable focus. Healthwise, you'll find your weight normalizing. Aches and pains you might have had to suffer with for years will gradually and steadily disappear. Being "sick" will become a rare event and seldom last for more than a day or two — and you will usually know what it was (i.e., what you ate) that made you sick. And, like me, you may find yourself "mysteriously" healing from diseases that the medical profession has no answers for. Raw living foods are simply amazing rejuvenating agents.

In my food classes, I suggest that everyone set a goal of eating at least 50% living and raw foods. As impossible as this may sound to you today, if you make the commitment to prepare at least one new recipe from this book every day, you will eventually reach this goal. You will find that the recipes are fun and easy to prepare, very delicious, and most importantly, will make you feel better than you can ever remember.

It may take two weeks, two months, or two years to get to 50%, depending on your motivation. Whatever the time, it doesn't matter — just do it. When I discovered all this, I knew why I had to start eating mostly living and raw food, and I did it virtually overnight. And am I ever grateful I chose to step up to life rather than continue to suffer and die slowly.

In the following chapters, we will take a closer look at what science is beginning to discover about living and raw foods, and then give you a vehicle and a roadmap that will help you transform your life and your health using the delicious, easy-to-prepare recipes that I have been blessed with creating while regaining my health.

Enzymes

The first new word I heard over and over as I began my study of living foods was "enzymes." I quickly learned that enzymes are types of protein catalysts that have to be present for life to exist. They perform a multitude of functions in the body, both metabolic and digestive. As an analogy that I easily understood when I heard it, an enzyme can be compared to a skilled worker who has been trained very well to perform a specific task. Without him, all work stops.

Enzymes appear in large numbers in living foods, slightly smaller numbers in raw foods, and do not exist in processed foods. This is because enzymes are very sensitive to heat. I learned that enzymes are one of the factors that give living foods their healing abilities. I also learned that enzyme quantities and activity levels in our bodies help determine how much energy we experience on any particular day.

Enzymes also play a vital role in the digestion, assimilation, and elimination of food and its by-products. Without enzymes, human life as we know it is not possible. And the more enzymes there are, the merrier we are.

Let's take a look at what happens enzymatically whenever we eat. While we're at it, try to remind yourself that each enzyme is a skilled worker best suited to perform a particular task but willing to attempt to fill in for other enzymes when necessary.

Let's say we're having lunch together. You've chosen a cooked entrée from the menu and I've decided to have a raw sprout salad. Within minutes after we start eating, an increasing number of enzymes appear in our digestive systems, especially our stomachs and upper small intestines. These enzymes play the very important role of breaking down our food. You may be asking yourself, "Where did the enzymes come from?" There are two possible sources: those in your food or those provided by your body.

Since your cooked entrée has zero enzymes, all of the enzymes for digestion have to be borrowed from your body's cells. This borrowing of enzymes also drains your body of its enzyme reserve. At birth, we are given a supply of enzymes, and they are not naturally replenished. Many of the maladies we associate with aging are actually symptoms of a diminishing enzyme reserve. Eating enzyme-rich living foods gets your body off the hook for that particular meal, letting the foods essentially digest themselves.

Remember that some of these borrowed enzymes are not "experts" in digestion — they were actually trained for other roles in your body. This creates two problems: your meal will be incompletely digested, which means you won't get all the nutrition possible, and the original task of those enzymes won't be completed.

Dr. Robert Young is a renowned microbiologist who has spent many years researching the relationship between mycotic infections (those started by yeast, fungus, and mold) and the onset of disease. Interestingly, he has discovered that if one's enzyme count drops below the level necessary to maintain a healthy cellular environment, a backup system activates dormant yeast and fungus spores in these cells, triggering a fermentation process as a self-defense mechanism. This is big, bad news for the body, and these underactive, "sick" cells use the body's endocrine relay system (sort of like our news media sources) to alert the body of this enzyme count drop. Unless the enzyme count can be restored to these cells in a timely fashion, they are eventually destroyed by the fermentation process, and unless the cells are removed, they become a source of toxicity in the body. More and more health professionals recognize this as a prominent source of sickness and disease in our societies today.

So, a first simple rule: as the enzyme levels in your body drop as a result of eating a meal of mostly processed food, so does your energy. Over the years, your body's ability to replace the enzymes that were recruited for digestion diminishes, and chronic ailments and diseases appear.

Quite a different picture develops as I'm eating my predominantly living/raw foods meal. Enzymes are abundant in the food. As a result, my digestive system doesn't need to borrow enzymes from my body to complete the digestive task at hand.

Meanwhile at the cellular level, my enzyme workforce remains high, meaning production of energy is maintained and the waste by-products of metabolism are removed efficiently. The result is that I feel light and full of energy even after eating a relatively large meal of living foods. (Some people mistakenly attribute this light feeling to not eating enough, because they are so conditioned to feeling sluggish after every meal. But after eating living foods for a month or so, you'll never want to go back to feeling like your "old self.") I noticed this change in me within days of starting to eat predominantly living foods.

Many "raw fooders" will argue, and I tend to agree with them, that raw living foods are more completely digested than processed foods. This results in better, more complete nutrition being delivered to your body's cells, and leaves behind fewer waste by-products to be removed.

Perhaps the most extensive research on the effect that food enzymes have on our health was conducted by Dr. Edward Howell, and documented in his easy-to-read book, *Enzyme Nutrition*. He found that people eating a lifetime of low-enzyme foods eventually drained their enzyme supply and became prone to digestive problems, premature aging, mineral and vitamin deficiencies, blood sugar imbalances, allergies, frequent illnesses, problems with their weight, osteoporosis, heart and circulatory diseases, and various forms of cancer. And the list goes on.

He also found that you could rebuild your enzyme supply by eating foods high in enzymes (i.e., raw living foods). His discoveries led him to create the first digestive enzyme supplements. Similar products are now widely available in health food stores. Though I feel these enzyme products can be of value to you as you transition your diet, I remind you that they are similar to your body's enzymes in that they are less than perfectly suited to digesting many of the foods you might eat. They do, however, reduce the drain on your cells' enzyme reserves.

In the end, a combination of raw and living foods with their natural enzymes intact will serve you best in your quest for optimum health throughout your life. The recipes in this book will show you how.

Body Chemistry 101: Alkaline and Acid

As scientific techniques to observe the cells of our bodies have improved over the past several decades, researchers have discovered that health and disease have very different chemistries in the human body. This is why a doctor often recommends a blood test be done when a patient is not feeling well.

The overall chemistry of a healthy human is slightly alkaline. Dr. Ted Morter, in his book *Your Health…Your Choice* explains it this way: "Your body is alkaline by design and acid-producing by function." When a person's overall chemistry becomes more acidic, he gradually loses his vitality and health. Realizing this, the medical/pharmaceutical world has looked for ways to restore alkalinity to the body. Most of today's medicines are in fact very alkaline substances that when taken in small doses do temporarily adjust the body's chemistry. This includes antacids and aspirin, two of the most commonly consumed over-the-counter products available. Unfortunately, their effects are short-lived and have side effects that often compound the health issue being addressed.

Changing your diet and introducing an abundance of living foods provide a much safer alternative than medicine in restoring the body's alkalinity. Let's look at why this is so. I'll try to make it simple so both you and I can understand it.

Consider any cell in your body to function like an alkaline battery. That is to say, there are areas in your cells that are designed to collect positive charges and areas that collect negative charges. Now, you might remember from your high school chemistry or physics class that opposite charges attract, or more specifically that the negative charges rush toward the positive charges. This is what we call electricity. So your body's cells in a healthy state produce steady minute pulses of electricity. It's always happening as long as these opposite charges exist in the body. Are you surprised? This is why you can be hooked up to an EKG machine and electrical impulses register on the meter.

Now the question: why do these areas of opposite charge exist? For life to go on, of course. But is there a condition in the cell that allows this to happen? Yes, and I'm glad you asked. The cells in our bodies can be compared to an ocean of chemical elements. Some of these elements are alkaline in nature; others are acidic. The most common alkaline elements in the body are calcium, sodium, potassium, magnesium, and iron. The common acidic elements include chlorine, iodine, sulfur, and phosphorus. The significance of this is that the alkaline elements attract the negative charges referred to above and the acid elements attract the positive charges. As long as these elements are available to hold these charges, electrical impulses are created, life goes on, and you're healthy and enjoying life.

So what happens when we get sick? Remember I started this chapter by mentioning that researchers have discovered that healthy cells are slightly alkaline. This means they have more alkaline elements than acid elements. When we become sick, it indicates that the cells in our bodies have become low in the alkaline elements, meaning there are fewer places in our cells to hold the necessary negative charges that create the electrical impulses of life. How this happens is simple. The source of all the elements in our body is…our diet. Admittedly, some come through the air we breathe, most importantly oxygen, but the majority come through the food we eat.

Years ago, studies were done to determine the composition of various foods and their overall acid-alkaline balance. You can find this information in many health books available today. And I invite you to do so if this interests you (see Recommended Reading). What you'll find is simple and very eye-opening: *with few exceptions, all raw vegetables and orchard-ripened fruits are alkaline; all other foods are acidic.* Notice I specify orchard-ripened fruit. This is important, because fruit that has been forced to ripen off of the tree can be acidic. It's the tree-ripening process that turns the fruit from acidic to alkaline. Don't ask me how — it's a miracle of life and it just happens. Now think of your diet over the years. What balance of alkaline to acid foods, by weight, have you eaten? So, is there any question why we feel the way we do so often?

The truth is that so many of us have grown up on a diet that is predominantly acid-forming in the body. Over the years, this has eroded the alkaline foundation that we were all born with. This has contributed greatly to our slow energy decline and the eventual health challenges that face us.

When you commit to changing your diet and adding living and raw foods to your meals, you will reverse this imbalance. A goal to set if you want your diet to provide you with the greatest health benefit is 80% alkaline, 20% acid. That is, 80% uncooked vegetables, nuts, seeds, beans, and grains and tree-ripened fruit, 20% other. Even though this seems like a daunting task when you first start out, you can think of it as a millionaire once said to me: you become a millionaire one dollar at a time, but you have to have the goal to achieve it. So you gradually change your diet one food and recipe at a time with the 80:20 ratio as your goal.

Raw living foods are so powerfully rejuvenative because they contain the elements to rebuild the alkaline reserves in our cells. They are loaded with calcium, sodium, potassium, magnesium, and iron. Even the nuts, seeds, grains, and beans that we use are either soaked in water for a determined amount of time or sprouted. This converts them from acid-forming to alkaline-forming when metabolized in the body's cells.

Another thing to note is that cooking your food makes it more acidic. In actuality, when you cook your vegetables or fruits, you lose some of their alkaline properties due to the chemical changes that occur during the cooking process.

There's an interesting sidebar to all of this alkaline/acid story, and it relates to our cellular enzymes that we discussed in the previous chapter. Enzyme activity is directly related to the chemistry of your cells. Is it any surprise that enzymes perform best when your cells' chemistry is slightly alkaline? When your cells' alkaline reserves diminish due to food choices, the enzymes slow down and you become tired.

The recipes in this book have been created to help restore the alkalinity in your cells so that you can begin to experience more of the spark that life has to offer. So don't delay — begin today to add more raw living foods to your diet by using the recipes in this book, and add more happiness to your life.

Dehydrated Foods

Surrendering our favorite cooked foods is one of the greatest challenges that most of us experience when we start moving into the living food arena. We've usually eaten these cooked foods for so long that we associate them with providing warmth and comfort to us, and they feel safe and nurturing. Even though they may not be the healthiest for us, we have come to truly enjoy their taste and their texture.

On a more subtle energy level, our bodies have taken on and resonate with the frequencies of these foods. When we attempt to stop eating them, our bodies become "starved" of these frequencies, especially if we are not including new foods that contain these frequencies, and we experience a craving.

One of the benefits of the recipes in this book is that they diminish these cravings for most of the people who have tested them for me. I feel it is very important that when we transition to living foods, we are getting all the nutrients that we need and we are completely satisfied.

One of the best ways to address this transition away from cooked foods is to have dehydrated foods around the house, especially for snacks. By learning how to prepare dehydrated foods, you can replicate most of the sensations that cooked foods provide, especially warmth and a familiar texture, without destroying the benefits of living and raw foods, especially the enzymes and oxygen.

Dehydrating is simply a method of warming and preparing food at a relatively low temperature (below 120 degrees Fahrenheit, if you want to retain the enzymes). If you live in a hot, dry climate, you can use the sun to do the dehydration, and this is actually practiced in many parts of the world. However, for most of us, this is not possible, especially during the winter months.

As a result, companies have created inexpensive machines called dehydrators with controlled heating elements and fans that allow you to dry vegetables, fruits, and any living foods creations you might come up with, including crackers and cookies, in your kitchen. You can find these machines in many department stores around the country.

Dehydrators produce high-energy foods that are crunchy and very tasty. Whenever I have leftovers or if I have too much of any kind of fresh foods, I place them in my dehydrator and I am often amazed with the results. I have dedicated an entire chapter in this book to these kinds of foods. I hope you do have fun playing with these recipes and that they trigger your imagination to come up with your very own special treats. Again, I feel dehydrated foods play an important role as one transitions away from cooked foods toward raw living foods.

Shopping & Selecting Organic Food

Before you can prepare any of the recipes in this book, you must first obtain all of the necessary ingredients. This naturally leads to the question of where to shop for the freshest and healthiest produce possible. As I have already suggested, the best place to find the most alive produce is in a garden where you can pick just what you need and leave the rest for a later time. This way, you let nature keep your food in its most vital state.

The second best source for quality produce is a farmers' market. If you don't know whether your community has a farmers' market, you can call your chamber of commerce for this information. Most of time, the smaller growers are there selling their pickings of the day at prices lower than you could get at retail stores. This gives you an opportunity to question them about what they use to fertilize their crops and whether they use pesticides of any sort. If possible, you should look for farmers who use no artificial fertilizers or pesticides, but rather who add compost and a natural mineral-rich amendment (containing up to 90 minerals) to their soil.

Compost, as most of you know, is a mixture of soil and decomposed vegetable scraps. It's a rich source of most nutrients, with the exception of essential minerals. This is the reason for the mineral-rich amendment, commonly referred to as rock dust, a pulverized rock that has been determined to have a full spectrum of essential minerals, especially the alkaline ones. Without these amendments, our soil becomes depleted within a few short years, and the crops grown on this soil then lack the essential nutrients we need to stay healthy. Again, our soils "bank" our foods' nutrients and need to have "deposits" made to them to allow yearly "withdrawals" to be made.

If you can't get everything you need from a home garden or

farmers' market, your next best shopping option is a natural food store or co-op. These kinds of stores are appearing in more and more cities and towns around the country as the consumer demand for organically grown food increases. They usually carry a wide range of organic fresh and dry produce. I suggest you purchase organically grown produce when possible. The trick in these stores is to get the freshest produce possible. You can do this by asking the produce manager when they get their deliveries and shop on these days. The drawbacks to natural foods stores and co-ops are that most of the produce is several days old before it reaches the shelves and the produce manager can't tell you the conditions the produce was grown under.

I realize that most Americans still do the bulk of their shopping at the local supermarket. This is fine. The most important thing is that you buy the freshest and healthiest looking produce possible. Recently, there has been a movement in many of the larger chains to add some organic products to their produce and dry bulk sections. If this hasn't happened at your supermarket, it might help if you were to suggest this to the produce manager. If he gets enough requests, he will probably accommodate you. His real concern will be whether he can stay profitable stocking these items. Usually, the managers are willing to start by stocking those vegetables that have the longest shelf life and aren't priced significantly higher than the conventional produce.

When you go to select your fresh produce, there are a few simple guidelines that I find work for me every time. Appearance and color are the first things I look for — produce that has a glow to it, indicating that it is relatively freshly picked. Bypass anything wilted or unusually wrinkled. Next, I use my sense of smell to determine whether the produce, especially fruit, has the nutritional value that I am looking for. In the case of vegetables, I will often sample a piece of the vegetable if there is no detectable aroma and yet it looks appealing. (One thing to note is that if the produce is cooled, it will not give off a strong scent even though it may be fully nutritious.) Finally, I will hold the produce in my hand. I've come to learn how the different vegetables and fruits should feel. And you will too if you haven't already mastered this. If the item is appealing to the eye, the nose, and the hand, it's in my basket.

At this point, it should make sense to you to shop for your fresh produce as often as possible so that it is as fresh as can be. The same to a lesser degree can be said for the dry good items like seeds, beans, nuts, and grains. It's important that these items are kept as cool as possible without freezing to retain their life force as long as possible and to slow the deterioration of their oils. I refrigerate as many of these as I can, and it makes a difference in their shelf life. I try never to purchase more than I will use within three months. Unless, of course, I get such a great deal that I'm willing to take the chance that I can use them up or give them away before they go bad.

So that's essentially it. Now it's time to choose a couple of recipes that appeal to you, prepare a shopping list, and use any new information I've given to help you shop. Then, come home and jump right into preparing at least one dish. And remember, have fun.

Healthy Living Foods
Need Healthy Living Soils!

While learning why living foods are so important we should also understand why healthy, living, fertile soil is vitally important. This brief chapter may serve as a reminder of this and to introduce the "remineralization" concept to readers unfamiliar with it.

Organic agriculture has long emphasized the need to return organic matter such as compost to the soil, and all compost ingredients have some minerals in them. But to generously remineralize soil with the full spectrum of elements found in the world's richest soils, it is necessary to also restore the rock minerals from which soil is originally derived. "The rock is the mother of the soil" is how one geologist of the 1800s put it. Since the most fertile soils usually have a variety of types of "parent rocks," it seems wise to try to duplicate the natural process when we remineralize. The Hunza Valley soils, for example, have grown some of the best crops of fruits and vegetables for centuries, and those fields are irrigated two or more times per year with the glacial gravel dust found in the Ultar Glacier meltwater, which they treasure as "glacial milk." Glacial action has produced much of the Earth's fertility. Glaciers grind and mix together a wide variety of rocks with diverse element content as they work over large areas with their crushing mass. Some volcanically derived soils such as those in Java can also be very fertile, although it is the areas like Hunza and Vilcabamba where glacial and alluvial (river-carried) soils form from mixed rock types, producing the "legendary" longevity found there.

To consciously begin your symbiotic relationship with the Earth by planting orchards and gardens is a direct, radical step toward total perfect health for the Earth — and for you as a caring, intelligent part of the Earth. As your caring translates to giving wisely and generously to soil and Earth, Nature responds with the beautiful, pure, vibrant living foods we need for real human health, thus completing this sacred symbiotic relationship cycle.

If you aren't aware how strongly and urgently the Earth and humanity are crying out for this "win-win" relationship, it only takes a little time and study — or simple observation — to become painfully aware of humanity's local/global confusion and "relationship problems!"

Remineralization feeds the soil microbes and worms the essential minerals they require to build their protoplasm and enzymes. If we want mineral and enzyme-rich live foods then we need to ensure that we or those who grow our food have provided these soil workers ("the real farmers," some have noted) their complete natural diet: organic compost, mulch, etc. and rock minerals. If you can do this in your own garden and orchard and eat fresh, living, mineralized produce, you can give thanks because you're living in Paradise!

Not quite, you say? Perhaps you can't help seeing how most people are unhealthy, the air is unnaturally visible, the water is in trouble, the forests are on their way out, the weather and climate are changing.

You may be right. A small island of paradise isn't the Paradise we know the earth is meant to be and can be. However, it is something we can all create if we set our hearts and hands to it. And it may be the best and only way to reverse the degenerative spiral toward Paradise Lost and to help our fellows glimpse how near Paradise Restored can really be. Never underestimate the power of an enzyme! Or the spirit of love when given to Mother Nature and to her human children. A taste of super-delicious living food from rich remineralized soil is one way to offer that "glimpse" — and there are few things more inspiring and soul-nourishing than a garden and orchard in bloom and fruition.

This chapter was written by Don Weaver, a gardener-ecologist-writer-networker who with John Hamaker co-authored *The Survival of Civilization*. Don helps produce *Remineralize the Earth* magazine, and is helping establish "Earth Regeneration Centers" and farms worldwide. He has thrived on a 100% organic living food diet for 22 years and radiates health.

To learn more, contact Don Weaver at:

Hamaker-Weaver Publishers
P. O. Box 1961-LIVE
Burlingame, CA 94011
(650) 347-9693

Soaking & Sprouting

If you're new to living foods, you've probably never considered soaking or sprouting your own supply of "fresh live produce." And at first you may be inclined for convenience to purchase as many of your sprouts as you can. However, I definitely recommend learning how to soak and sprout as much of your food as possible. Why? It's extremely economical. It takes very little time and is very easy. They're as fresh as possible, and you know no pesticides and chemicals have been added. Sprouts are easy to digest, and are rich sources of oxygen, enzymes, vitamins, and essential minerals. As a result, they are perfect additions to most of the main dishes, patés, salads, and soups that you will be learning to prepare.

In general, all raw nuts need only be soaked 12 hours before they are ready to use. All seeds, grains, and beans can be used after they have been softened through soaking, but are best soaked and then sprouted for one to five days. This is especially true of the small seeds like alfalfa and clover that will produce two green leaves, rich in chlorophyll, after four or five days of sprouting.

Guidelines for Sprouting

♥ **Dry storage:** store your raw nuts, seeds, grains, and beans in sealed containers in a cool, dry location (a refrigerator is the best). This lengthens their storage life.

♥ **Soaking:** all raw nuts, seeds, grains, and beans are brought to life when placed in water, which dissolves their enzyme inhibitors. Unless otherwise specified, purified room-temperature water is best. You can do the soaking wherever you have the room and the temperature is comfortable for you. Small seeds like alfalfa and clover, and small grains like quinoa and millet should be soaked for around 5 hours. Hulled seeds like sunflower and pumpkin become soft after 6 to 8 hours. And large grains like wheat and rye; beans like mung, garbanzos, and lentils; and nuts like almonds and walnuts usually become softened, and in the case of the grains and beans, are ready to germinate in about 12 hours. The soaking can be done in any nonmetal container — I like to use glass jars so that I can watch the sprouts grow. I cover the jars with a piece of nylon screen, wire mesh, or cotton cheesecloth held in place by a rubber band. This makes rinsing them very easy. All soaked items should be rinsed every 6 to 8 hours and new water should added.

After soaking, nuts can be rinsed, new water added, and they can be used or placed in the refrigerator until you are ready to use them. The water should be changed every two to three days, as they are alive and produce waste that gets in the water.

♥ **Germination:** after soaking, the seeds, grains, and beans are drained and rinsed well, and put back in their containers. At this point, it's important to understand that they need to be kept moist but not wet, they must be able to breathe (which the nylon screen, wire mesh, or cheesecloth allows), and they want to be kept in the dark (as if they had been planted in the ground) at a comfortable room temperature. Good places to consider for the germination are in a closet, under a towel, or in a covered box. During this stage, it's important to rinse your "babies" twice a day. I usually do this in the morning when I wake up and in the evening before I retire. This way, they are cleaned and refreshed.

Everything except the small seeds (alfalfa, clover, radish, cabbage, etc.) are ready to harvest when the sprout becomes as long as the seed out of which it grew. This usually happens within one to four days. These "ripe" sprouts can then be washed and drained well one last time before they join your nuts in the refrigerator.

♥   **Greening:** the final stage for the small seeds begins when you see the first sign of two small leaves appearing. At this point, place them in indirect light so that they can begin the greening process, producing the chlorophyll that is so healing to us. Caring for them at this stage is the same as during germination: rinse and drain well every 12 hours.

After one or two days, the leaves on these sprouts turn green and they are ready to be harvested. At this point, you may want to put them in a bowl and wash away the hulls that have separated from the sprouts. This keeps the sprouts fresher for a longer period of time in your refrigerator. After you've rinsed the sprouts, be sure to drain them well before putting them in the refrigerator for storage.

Most sprouts will last for at least a week in the refrigerator, especially if they are rinsed and drained well every three days.

These soaked and sprouted truly living foods have many uses. Soaked nuts and sunflower and pumpkin seeds are wonderful to use in making delicious milks, patés, salad dressings, dehydrated snacks, and pie crusts. Sprouted grains are great in milks, dehydrated breads & crackers, and as a cereal. Sprouted beans add great nutrition and a distinct quality to your salads, casseroles, and breads. And the green sprouts from the small seeds with their inherent life force are great salad toppers. They can also be used in your raw vegetable juices.

The more you experiment with these true living foods, the more you will feel their vitality filling your mind and body with their wonderful energies. Enjoy the delight that they provide.

Soaking and Sprouting Procedure

Step 1
Put measured seeds, nuts, grains, or legumes into a fine-mesh colander and rinse. Then put them into a glass jar and cover them with pure water three to four inches above the seeds. Let the seeds soak overnight or for the specified time. The water awakens the plant enzymes within the seeds, triggering the life force that begins the sprouting cycle.

Step 2
Place a mesh on the top of the glass jar to prevent seeds from rinsing away. Drain away soak water (and hulls). This will discard the enzyme inhibitors. Rinse the seeds with pure water, then drain again.

Step 3
Let your seeds rest in the glass jar on the kitchen counter under a towel (or another dark place) for 12 to 24 hours. Keep jars at a 45° angle for the best drainage. Rinse and drain twice a day until the desired sprout tails appear.

Step 4
Expose your sprouts to sunlight for about six hours to activate the abundance of chlorophyll. Enjoy!

Living in the Raw

Sprouting Chart

Plant Variety	Amount of Seed for Quart Jar	Soaking Time (hrs)	Rinses Per Day
Adzuki bean	1/2 C	12	2
Alfalfa	2 T	6	2
Buckwheat groats	1 C	8–14	2
Cabbage	3 T	4–6	2
Chickpeas (garbanzo beans)	1 C	12	2
Chinese cabbage	3 T	12	2
Clover	2 T	6	2
Corn	1 1/2 C	10–14	2
Fenugreek	1/4 C	8	2
Flax*		4–6	-
Lentil	3/4 C	8–12	2
Lettuce	3 T	6	2
Mung bean	1/2 C	12	2
Mustard	3 T	6	2
Oat groats	1 1/2 C	8–12	2
Pea	2 C	8	2
Peanut	1 C	8	2
Pumpkin	1 1/2 C	8	2
Quinoa	1/3 C	4–8	2
Radish	3 T	4–8	2
Rye	1 C	12	2
Sesame seeds	2 C	4–6	2
Soybeans	3/4 C	8	2
Wheat (hard)	1 C	8	2
Wheat (soft)	1 C	8	2

*Flax seeds are sprouted by soaking in a bowl for 4 to 6 hours. Do not rinse.

Blanching Almonds

Place almonds soaked for 12 to 48 hours (and rinsed every 12 hours) in a bowl. Pour boiling water over almonds and let sit for no more than 30 seconds to 1 minute. Drain boiling water, and pour cool water over almonds. Pop skins off using your middle finger, index finger and thumb, and place blanched almonds in another bowl.

Setting up a Raw Living Food Kitchen

Setting up a raw living food kitchen is simple and enjoyable. You may already have much of this equipment in your kitchen. If not, you can find them in health food stores, kitchen stores, catalogues, the Internet, and department stores. Some of the equipment may be unfamiliar, but none of them are difficult to learn and use. Simply follow the manufacturer's instructions and the recipes in this book. The following is a list of items that are useful in a raw living food kitchen.

I have also listed many of the common bulk foods and seasonings you should have on hand when preparing the recipes in this book.

Equipment

- dehydrator
- dish rack (for sprouting)
- food processor
- heavy-duty blender
- juicer (electric)
- small hand (citrus) juicer
- small, medium, & large bowls
- colander
- wooden cutting board
- small, medium & large funnels
- glass pitcher
- glass storage containers
- grater
- knives

- mandolin (hand-slicer)
- small, medium & large mason jars
- 8″ springform pan
- pie plates
- small, medium & large platters
- rectangular glass pans
- small hand food chopper
- small, medium & large glass storage jars
- spice jars
- strainer
- wire or nylon mesh or cheesecloth

Utensils

- measuring cups
- measuring spoons
- rubber spatulas
- spatulas

- thermometer
- vegetable scrub brush
- wooden spoons
- zester

Bulk Foods

Beans

- adzuki beans
- garbanzo beans
- lentils

- mung beans
- soybeans

Dried Fruits

- dates
- dehydrated bananas
- mission figs

- raisins
- shredded coconut
- sun-dried tomatoes

Grains

- barley
- buckwheat groats
- quinoa

- oat groats
- rye
- soft wheat berries

Nuts

- almonds
- hazelnuts
- pecans

- pine nuts
- walnuts

Seeds

- flax seeds
- pumpkin seeds

- sesame seeds
- sunflower seeds

Flavorings

- almond extract
- coconut extract
- pure vanilla

Seasonings

- basil
- Bragg Liquid Aminos
- cardamom
- caraway seeds
- cayenne
- chili
- chervil
- cilantro
- cinnamon
- cloves
- coriander
- cumin
- cumin seeds
- curry
- dill weed
- ginger
- Italian seasonings
- kelp
- marjoram
- mustard
- nutmeg
- oregano
- paprika
- parsley
- sage
- savory
- tarragon
- turmeric
- thyme

Oils

- extra virgin olive oil
- flax oil

Other

- raw tahini
- psyllium powder

Three Months to a Healthier Mind, Body and Soul

1st week:

- ♥ Eliminate all saturated fats. Use only uncooked organic cold-pressed virgin olive oil or flax oil.

- ♥ Eliminate all red meat, white flour, white sugar, and processed foods.

- ♥ Eat only organic fruits and vegetables.

- ♥ Exercise for 10 minutes three days this week (walking, biking, swimming, tennis, whatever will get you excited about exercising).

- ♥ Keep a diary of your progress and how you feel about your new lifestyle.

- ♥ Spend 10 minutes a day by yourself in a quiet space free of thoughts and listen to the little voice inside. What is it telling you?

- ♥ Spend a total of 10 minutes in the sun before 10 AM or after 2 PM every day. Expose as much of your body as possible.

2nd week:

- ♥ Make one day this week a vegetarian day.

- ♥ Locate a farmers' market in your area and buy as much of your food from local organic farmers as possible. The food is fresher, less expensive and healthier.

- ♥ Do something special for yourself. You made it through the first week!

♥ Exercise for 15 minutes three days this week.

♥ Don't forget to write in your diary!

♥ Spend 15 minutes a day meditating, preferably first thing in the morning, and make it part of your daily routine.

♥ Spend a total of 15 minutes in the sun before 10 AM or after 2 PM every day. Expose as much of your body as possible.

3rd week:

♥ Make two days this week vegan days. (Eliminate all dairy and other animal products on these days.)

♥ Call someone you haven't seen or talked to in a long time.

♥ Exercise for 20 minutes three days this week.

♥ Buy yourself some flowers. Farmers' markets usually have flowers at very reasonable prices.

♥ Spend a total of 20 minutes in the sun before 10 AM or after 2 PM every day. Expose as much of your body as possible.

♥ Continue writing in your diary throughout this program.

4th week:

♥ Make three days this week vegan days.

♥ Read a book about health (recommended: *Conscious Eating* by Gabriel Cousens, MD).

♥ Do something special for a friend.

♥ Exercise for 30 minutes three days this week.

♥ Spend a total of 25 minutes in the sun before 10 AM or after 2 PM every day. Expose as much of your body as possible.

♥ Treat yourself to a massage.

Three Months

5th week:

- ♥ Make four days this week vegan days.

- ♥ Continue reading books.

- ♥ Do something special for someone you don't know.

- ♥ Exercise for 45 minutes three days this week.

- ♥ Buy yourself some flowers. Take time to smell the roses and to see the beauty in flowers.

- ♥ Spend a total of 30 minutes in the sun before 10 AM or after 2 PM every day. Expose as much of your body as possible.

6th week:

- ♥ Make five days this week vegan days.

- ♥ Continue reading books.

- ♥ Go on a hike in nature with a friend.

- ♥ Exercise for 45 minutes four days this week.

- ♥ Spend at least 30 minutes in the sun every day for the rest of your life.

7th week:

- ♥ Make six days this week vegan days.

- ♥ Read *The Wheatgrass Book* by Ann Wigmore

- ♥ Give back to your community and volunteer!

- ♥ Exercise for 45 minutes five days this week. Congratulations! You are now on your exercise program for the rest of your life. Be sure to take the time — you deserve it!

- ♥ Buy yourself some flowers.

8th week:

- ♥ Make every day this week a vegan day. Congratulations! You are now a full-time vegan, eating only fruits, vegetables, nuts, and seeds.

- ♥ Read *Fasting Can Save Your Life* by Herbert Shelton.

- ♥ Buy some flowers for someone special in your life.

- ♥ Start on a wheatgrass program. Begin with 1 oz. each day, and increase when your body tells you to.

- ♥ Treat yourself to a massage.

9th week:

- ♥ Eat two raw living foods meals for two days this week.

- ♥ Learn about juicing. Maybe buy a juicer, and start including juice in your diet.

- ♥ Buy some flowers and give them to someone you don't know.

- ♥ Perhaps this is the week you think about doing a fast, just for a day, maybe on vegetable juice and water or just water.

- ♥ Buy yourself some flowers.

10th week:

- ♥ Eat two raw living foods meals for three days this week.

- ♥ Read a book.

- ♥ Volunteer in your community!

Three Months

11th week:

- ♥ Eat two raw living foods meals for four days this week.
- ♥ Read a book.
- ♥ Volunteer!
- ♥ Buy yourself some flowers.

12th week:

- ♥ Eat two raw living foods meals for five days this week.
- ♥ Read a book.
- ♥ Volunteer!
- ♥ Treat yourself to a massage.

13th week:

- ♥ Eat two raw living foods meals for six days this week.
- ♥ Read a book.
- ♥ Buy yourself some flowers.

14th week:

- ♥ Eat two raw living foods meals every day this week. Continue to include more raw living foods in your diet. Ultimately, you should try to maintain 80 to 100% raw living foods.
- ♥ Continue reading books that interest you and expand your mind, body and soul.
- ♥ Continue to treat yourself to flowers — you deserve it.
- ♥ Read your diary and notice the changes in your life.

Appetizers

Avocado Dulse Dip

1	avocado, chopped
1 T	dulse flakes
1 T	lemon juice
1 T	Bragg Liquid Aminos
1/4 t	chili powder
3	green onions, finely chopped

In a blender, mix avocado, dulse, lemon juice, Bragg, and chili powder. Stir in green onions.

Appetizers

Basil Pesto

3 C   fresh basil

½ C   sunflower seeds, soaked 6 hours and rinsed

2 T   lemon juice

2–4   cloves garlic, minced

1 T   Bragg Liquid Aminos

1   tomato, chopped

Process basil, sunflower seeds, lemon juice, garlic, and Bragg in a food processor with the "s" blade, and pulse chop several times. Stop to scrape down the sides, and repeat until the mixture is smooth. Add tomatoes and continue to pulse chop until just blended.

Bean Dip

2 C   lentils, sprouted

2 T   raw tahini

2 T   lemon juice

1 T   Bragg Liquid Aminos

1 t   chili powder

1 t   cumin

fresh garlic (optional)

Process lentils through a Champion Juicer using the solid plate or a food processor using the "s" blade. Add remaining ingredients and mix well.

Appetizers

Carrot Salsa

2 carrots, grated

1/2 red onion, diced

1/4 C mild peppers, finely chopped

2 t Bragg Liquid Aminos

1 t lime juice

1 clove garlic, minced (optional)

Mix all ingredients together in a bowl. Serve with your favorite crackers or vegetable chips.

Cocktail Nuts

1 T   flax oil

1 t   Bragg Liquid Aminos

2 – 4   cloves garlic, minced

½   yellow onion, juiced

1 C   almonds, soaked 12 – 48 hours and blanched

1 C   hazelnuts, soaked 6 – 8 hours

1 C   pumpkin seeds, soaked 6 – 8 hours

1 C   walnuts, soaked 6 – 8 hours

Mix flax oil, Bragg, garlic, and onion juice together in a large bowl. Add nuts and toss well. Place nuts on a dehydrator tray at 105° for 8 – 10 hours or until desired crispness is obtained.

Appetizers

Guacamole

4	avocados
1	red bell pepper
½	yellow onion
2	cloves garlic, minced
1 T	lime juice
2 t	Bragg Liquid Aminos
⅛ t	cayenne

Process avocados in a food processor using the "s" blade until creamy and pour into bowl. Pulse chop bell pepper, onion, and garlic until chunky. Fold into avocado mixture. Add lime juice, Bragg, and cayenne.

Jerusalem Artichoke Chips

1 lb   Jerusalem artichokes

Scrub Jerusalem artichokes, and slice into uniform thin rounds by running through handheld slicer or with a knife. Dehydrate at 105° for 3 – 6 hours, or until desired crispness is obtained. Jerusalem artichokes can be eaten raw, thinly sliced as "chips" or tossed in salads.

Red Bell Pepper Salsa

6   red bell peppers, finely chopped

1   bunch cilantro, chopped

1   red onion, finely chopped

1   clove garlic, minced

2 T lemon juice

1 T Bragg Liquid Aminos

Mix all ingredients in a large bowl and serve.

Salsa

4	firm tomatoes, finely chopped
1	red bell pepper, finely chopped
1	yellow onion, finely chopped
1	medium anaheim or poblano chili pepper, finely chopped
1/2–1	jalapeño or serrano chili, finely chopped
2	cloves garlic, minced
1/3 C	fresh cilantro, finely chopped
2–3 T	lemon juice
2 t	Bragg Liquid Aminos

Combine all ingredients in a large bowl. Cover and refrigerate to allow the flavors to mix.

Appetizers

Spinach Dip

1 lb   spinach, washed

½ C   yellow onions, chopped

½ C   raw tahini

1   clove garlic, minced

½   cucumber juice

3 T   lemon juice

2 T   flax oil

1 t   Bragg Liquid Aminos

½ t   dried dill weed

⅛ t   cayenne

Process spinach, onions, tahini, and garlic in a food processor using the "s" blade until smooth and pour into a bowl. Add remaining ingredients and mix well. Add water if consistency is too thick.

Spinach Herb Dip

1 lb	spinach, washed
1	avocado
1¼ C	parsley
¾ C	fresh dill sprigs
2 T	dry mustard
1 T	raw tahini
1 T	Bragg Liquid Aminos
1 T	dried Italian seasoning

Process all ingredients in a food processor using "s" blade until smooth.

Appetizers

Stuffed Mushrooms

Stuffing:

1/3 C   pine nuts

3   cloves garlic, minced

1/3 C   fresh cilantro, packed leaves, chopped

1/3 C   fresh basil, packed leaves, chopped

1 T   lemon juice

2 t   Bragg Liquid Aminos

1 C   tomato, chopped

12   large mushrooms

Process all ingredients except the tomatoes in a food processor using the "s" blade. Pulse chop several times. Stop to scrape down the sides and repeat. Add the tomatoes and continue to pulse chop until just blended. Texture should be thick, not a purée. Remove stems from mushrooms, and stuff the filling into the cap of the mushroom. Place on a dehydrator tray and dehydrate at 105° for 2 – 4 hours.

Sunflower Seeds

4 C   sunflower seeds, soaked 6 – 8 hours and rinsed

½ C Bragg Liquid Aminos

After soaking sunflower seeds for 6 – 8 hours, rinse then pour Bragg over the sunflower seeds and marinate 6 – 8 hours in the refrigerator. Drain Bragg, and spread sunflower seeds on a dehydrator tray, making sure to spread evenly. Dehydrate at 105° for approximately 6 – 8 hours until sunflower seeds are completely dry and crispy. This makes a wonderful snack or addition to a salad for some crunch.

Tahini Dip

½ C   water

1 t   dry mustard

1 C   raw tahini

2   cloves garlic

½   beet

3 T   lemon juice

1 T   Bragg Liquid Aminos

In a small bowl, mix dry mustard powder with enough water to make a paste, and let sit at least 10 minutes. In a blender, or food processor with the "s" blade, process tahini, garlic, beet, and lemon juice. Add mustard and Bragg. You may need to use additional water for a thinner consistency. Store in glass jar. Use as a spread on crackers or as a dip for a vegetable tray.

Thai Tomato Salsa

6	large basil leaves, finely chopped
3	tomatoes, chopped
2	green onions, finely chopped
3–4	cloves garlic, minced
1/3 C	lemon juice
1/2 C	red onion, finely chopped
2 T	flax oil
2 T	virgin olive oil
1 T	ginger, peeled, and grated

Combine all ingredients in a large mixing bowl.

Appetizers

Tomato Avocado Salsa

3   tomatoes, chopped (about 1 C)

1   jalapeño chili, seeded and chopped

1/2   avocado, cut into small cubes

1/2   yellow bell pepper, chopped

3 T   fresh basil, chopped

2 T   red onion, chopped

1 T   lime juice

2 t   Bragg Liquid Aminos

Combine all ingredients in a bowl.

Yam Chips

3   sweet potatoes

Scrub sweet potatoes, and slice into uniform thin rounds by
running through handheld slicer. Dehydrate at 105° for 3 – 6 hours
until desired crispness is obtained.

Zucchini Chips

4   zucchini

Scrub zucchini, and slice into uniform thin rounds by running through handheld slicer. Dehydrate at 105° for 3 – 6 hours until desired crispness is obtained.

Breads

Muffins

&

Crackers

Apricot Almond Bread

2½ C soft wheat berries, sprouted 1 day

¼ C dried apricots, soaked and finely chopped

2 slices dried pineapple, soaked and finely chopped

1 C raw honey or 1 C honey dates

½ C almonds, soaked 12 – 48 hours, blanched and finely chopped

1 t vanilla

1 t orange zest

Process wheat through a Champion Juicer using the solid plate. Add apricots, pineapple, honey, almonds, vanilla, and orange zest to the wheat; mix well. Form into two loaves of bread. Place on a dehydrator tray with a teflex sheet, and dehydrate at 105° for 4 – 6 hours. Turn bread over, and remove teflex sheet. Continue dehydrating for 4 – 6 hours, or until desired moisture is obtained.

Banana Bread

2 C   soft wheat berries, sprouted 1 day

3   bananas

½ C   honey dates

1 t   vanilla

1 t   cinnamon

Process wheat, bananas, and dates through a Champion Juicer using the solid plate. Add vanilla and cinnamon; mix well. Form into two loaves of bread. Place on a dehydrator tray with a teflex sheet in the dehydrator at 105° for 4 – 6 hours. Turn bread over, and remove teflex sheet. Continue dehydrating for 4 – 6 hours, or until desired moisture is obtained.

Carrot Raisin Bread

3 C   soft wheat berries, sprouted 1 day

½ C honey dates

1 C   carrots, finely grated

1 C   raisins, soaked 1 hour

1 C   walnuts, chopped

1 t   cinnamon

¼ t   nutmeg

¼ t   cardamom

Process wheat and dates through a Champion Juicer using the solid plate. Add all remaining ingredients; mix well. Form into three loaves of bread. Place on a dehydrator tray with a teflex sheet, and dehydrate at 105° for 4 – 6 hours. Turn bread over, and remove teflex sheet. Continue dehydrating for 4 – 6 hours, or until desired moisture is obtained.

Cinnamon Date Bread

3 C   soft wheat berries, sprouted 1 day

1 C   honey dates

½ C   raisins

1 t   cinnamon

Process wheat and dates through a Champion Juicer using the solid plate. Add raisins, and cinnamon to the mixture; mix well. Form into three loaves of bread. Place on a dehydrator tray with a teflex sheet, and dehydrate at 105° for 4 – 6 hours. Turn bread over, and remove teflex sheet. Continue dehydrating for 4 – 6 hours, or until desired moisture is obtained.

Light Rye Bread

1 C   rye, sprouted 2 days

1 C   soft wheat berries, sprouted 1 day

½ C   honey dates

Process rye, wheat, and dates through a Champion Juicer using the solid plate and mix well. Form into two loaves of bread. Place on a dehydrator tray with a teflex sheet, and dehydrate at 105° for 4 – 6 hours. Turn bread over, and remove teflex sheet. Continue dehydrating for 4 – 6 hours, or until desired moisture is obtained.

Oatmeal Raisin Bread

2 C   oat groats, sprouted 2 – 3 days

1 C   soft wheat berries, sprouted 1 day

¼ C   honey dates

1 C   walnuts, soaked 6 hours and chopped

½ C   raisins

1 t   Bragg Liquid Aminos

Process oats, wheat, and dates through a Champion Juicer using the solid plate. Add all remaining ingredients; mix well. Form into three loaves of bread. Place on a dehydrator tray with a teflex sheet and dehydrate at 105° for 4 – 6 hours. Turn bread over, and remove teflex sheet. Continue dehydrating for 4 – 6 hours, or until desired moisture is obtained.

Pumpkin Bread

2 C   soft wheat berries, sprouted 1 day

1 C   barley, soaked 2 days

½ C   honey dates

1½ C fresh pumpkin

½   orange

½ C   raisins

½ C   walnuts, soaked 6 hours and chopped

1 t   orange zest

1 t   cinnamon

½ t   dry ginger

Process wheat, barley, and dates through a Champion Juicer using the solid plate. In a blender, purée pumpkin and orange; add to the mixture. Add raisins, walnuts, and spices; mix well. Form into three loaves of bread. Place on a dehydrator tray with a teflex sheet, and dehydrate at 105° for 4 – 6 hours. Turn bread over, and remove teflex sheet. Continue dehydrating for 4 – 6 hours, or until desired moisture is obtained.

Rye Bread

2 C rye, sprouted 2 days

¼ C dates

Process rye and dates through a Champion Juicer using the solid plate and mix well. Form into two loaves of bread. Place on a dehydrator tray with a teflex sheet, and dehydrate at 105° for 4 – 6 hours. Turn bread over, and remove teflex sheet. Continue dehydrating for 4 – 6 hours, or until desired moisture is obtained.

Wheat Bread

2 C   soft wheat berries, sprouted 1 day

½ C   honey dates

Process wheat and dates through a Champion Juicer using the solid plate; mix well. Form into two loaves of bread. Place on a dehydrator tray with a teflex sheet, and dehydrate at 105° for 4 – 6 hours. Turn bread over, and remove teflex sheet. Continue dehydrating for 4 – 6 hours, or until desired moisture is obtained.

Zucchini Bread

2 C   soft wheat berries, sprouted 1 day

1/2 C honey dates

1 C   zucchini, finely grated

1 C   raisins

1 t   vanilla

1 t   cinnamon

1/2 t fresh ground nutmeg

1/4 t cardamom

Process wheat and dates through a Champion Juicer using the solid plate. Add zucchini and remaining ingredients; mix well. Form into two loaves of bread. Place on a dehydrator tray with a teflex sheet, and dehydrate at 105° for 4 – 6 hours. Turn bread over, and remove teflex sheet. Continue dehydrating for 4 – 6 hours, or until desired moisture is obtained.

Apple Muffins

1 C   soft wheat berries, sprouted 1 day

1 C   barley, soaked 2 days

2   bananas

2 C   sweet apples, finely grated

3/4 C honey dates

1/2 C raisins

1 t   vanilla

1 t   cinnamon

1 C   pecans, soaked 6 hours and chopped

Process wheat, barley, bananas, apples, and dates through a Champion Juicer using the solid plate. Add raisins, vanilla, cinnamon, and pecans; mix well. Form into 6 round muffins approximately 3/4″ thick. Place on a dehydrator tray with a teflex sheet, and dehydrate at 105° for 4 hours. Turn muffins over, and remove teflex sheet. Continue dehydrating for 4 – 6 hours, or until desired moisture is obtained.

Apricot Muffins

1 C   soft wheat berries, sprouted 1 day

1 C   barley, soaked 2 days

8   dried apricots or 4 fresh

1   banana

3/4 C honey dates

1 t   vanilla

1 t   cinnamon

1 C   walnuts, soaked 6 hours and chopped

Process wheat, barley, banana, apricots (if using fresh), and dates through a Champion Juicer using the solid plate. Add finely chopped apricots (if using dried), vanilla, cinnamon, and walnuts; mix well. Form into 6 round muffins approximately 3/4″ thick. Place on a dehydrator tray with a teflex sheet, and dehydrate at 105° for 4 hours. Turn muffins over, and remove teflex sheet. Continue dehydrating for 4 – 6 hours, or until desired moisture is obtained.

Banana Muffins

1 C   soft wheat berries, sprouted 1 day

1 C   oats, sprouted 2 days

3   bananas

3/4 C   honey dates

1 t   vanilla

1 t   cinnamon

1 C   walnuts, soaked 6 hours and chopped

Process wheat, barley, bananas, and dates through a Champion Juicer using the solid plate. Add vanilla, cinnamon, and walnuts; mix well. Form into 6 round muffins approximately 3/4″ thick. Place on a dehydrator tray with a teflex sheet, and dehydrate at 105° for 4 hours. Turn muffins over, and remove teflex sheet. Continue dehydrating for 4 – 6 hours, or until desired moisture is obtained.

Muffins

Blueberry Muffins

1 C   soft wheat berries, sprouted 1 day

1 C   barley, soaked 2 days

2   bananas

3/4 C honey dates

1/2 C blueberries

1 t   vanilla

1 1/2 t cinnamon

Process wheat, barley, bananas, and dates through a Champion Juicer using the solid plate. Add blueberries, vanilla, and cinnamon; mix well. Form into 6 round muffins approximately 3/4" thick. Place on a dehydrator tray with a teflex sheet, and dehydrate at 105° for 4 hours. Turn muffins over, and remove teflex sheet. Continue dehydrating for 4 – 6 hours, or until desired moisture is obtained.

Breakfast Muffins

5 C buckwheat, sprouted

10 medjool dates

1 C golden currants

1 C walnuts, soaked 6 hours and chopped

2 t vanilla

Process buckwheat and dates through a Champion Juicer using the solid plate, alternating one after the other. Add golden currants, walnuts, and vanilla; mix well. Form into round muffins. Place on a dehydrator tray with a teflex sheet, and dehydrate at 105° for 4 – 6 hours. Turn muffins over, and remove teflex sheet. Continue dehydrating for 4 – 6 hours, or until desired moisture is obtained.

Carrot Raisin Muffins

1 C   soft wheat berries, sprouted 1 day

1 C   barley, soaked 2 days

3/4 C   honey dates

3/4 C   carrots, finely grated

1 C   raisins, soaked

1 t   cinnamon

1/4 t   cardamom

1/4 t   nutmeg

1 C   walnuts, soaked 6 hours and chopped

Process wheat, barley, and dates through a Champion Juicer using the solid plate. Add carrots, raisins, cinnamon, cardamom, nutmeg, and walnuts; mix well. Form into 6 round muffins approximately 3/4″ thick. Place on a dehydrator tray with a teflex sheet and dehydrate at 105° for 4 – 6 hours. Turn muffins over, and remove teflex sheet. Continue dehydrating for 4 – 6 hours, or until desired moisture is obtained.

Los Altos Scones

(Recipe by Pam Masters)

4 C   buckwheat, sprouted

2 C   raisins

½ C   raisins

1 C   walnuts, soaked 6 hours and chopped

1 t   vanilla

Process buckwheat and 2 C of raisins through the Champion Juicer using the solid plate, alternating one after the other. Stir in ½ C raisins, walnuts, and vanilla. Form into round biscuits. Place on a dehydrator tray with a teflex sheet, and dehydrate at 105° for 4 – 6 hours. Turn scones over, and remove teflex sheet. Continue to dehydrate for 4 – 6 hours, or until desired moisture is obtained.

Muffins

Peach Muffins

1 C   soft wheat berries, sprouted 1 day

1 C   barley, soaked 2 days

2   ripe peaches

3/4 C honey dates

1 t   vanilla

1 t   cinnamon

1/2 t fresh ground nutmeg

1 C   hazelnuts, soaked 6 hours and chopped

Process wheat, barley, peaches, and dates through a Champion Juicer using the solid plate. Add vanilla, cinnamon, nutmeg, and hazelnuts; mix well. Form into 6 round muffins approximately 3/4″ thick. Place on a dehydrator tray with a teflex sheet, and dehydrate at 105° for 4 hours. Turn muffins over, and remove teflex sheet. Continue dehydrating for 4 – 6 hours, or until desired moisture is obtained.

Persimmon Muffins

1 C	soft wheat berries, sprouted 1 day
1 C	barley, soaked 2 days
2	large persimmons
3/4 C	honey dates
1 C	raisins
1 C	walnuts, soaked 6 hours and chopped
1 t	cinnamon
1 t	vanilla

Process wheat, barley, persimmons, and dates through a Champion Juicer using the solid plate. Add raisins, walnuts, cinnamon, and vanilla; mix well. Form into 6 round muffins approximately 3/4″ thick. Place on a dehydrator tray with a teflex sheet and dehydrate at 105° for 4 hours. Turn muffins over, and remove teflex sheet. Continue dehydrating for 4 – 6 hours, or until desired moisture is obtained.

Muffins

Pineapple Orange Muffins

1 C   soft wheat berries, sprouted 1 day

1 C   barley, soaked 2 days

2   bananas

³/₄ C honey dates

4   rings dried pineapple, soaked 2 hours and finely chopped

1 C   walnuts, soaked 6 hours and chopped

3 T   orange zest

1 t   vanilla

Process wheat, barley, bananas, and dates through a Champion Juicer using the solid plate. Add pineapple, walnuts, orange zest, and vanilla; mix well. Form into 6 round muffins approximately ³/₄″ thick. Place on a dehydrator tray with a teflex sheet, and dehydrate at 105° for 4 hours. Turn muffins over, and remove teflex sheet. Continue dehydrating for 4 – 6 hours, or until desired moisture is obtained.

Zucchini Muffins

1 C   soft wheat berries, sprouted 1 day

1 C   barley, soaked 2 days

3/4 C honey dates

1 C   zucchini, finely grated and loosely packed

1 C   raisins

1 t   vanilla

1 t   cinnamon

1/4 t fresh ground nutmeg

Process wheat, barley, and dates through a Champion Juicer using the solid plate. Add zucchini, raisins, vanilla, cinnamon, and nutmeg; mix well. Form into 6 round muffins approximately 3/4″ thick. Place on a dehydrator tray with a teflex sheet, and dehydrate at 105° for 4 hours. Turn muffins over, and remove teflex sheet. Continue dehydrating for 4 – 6 hours, or until desired moisture is obtained.

Muffins

Corn Chips

(Recipe by Cynthia Juenemann)

6	ears corn, removed from cob
½	yellow onion
2 C	sunflower seeds, soaked 6 hours and rinsed
¼ C	water
1½ T	Bragg Liquid Aminos
1 t	kelp powder

Process corn and onion in a food processor using the "s" blade. Stop and scrape the sides; blend until smooth. Add sunflower seeds, and process until the mixture is well blended and the consistency of a batter. Add some water if the batter is too thick. Add Bragg and kelp; mix well. Using a teaspoon, scoop batter onto a dehydrator tray with a teflex sheet, and flatten with a table knife into a flat round surface about ⅛″ thick and 1½″ wide. Dehydrate at 105° for 12 hours, turn chips over, and remove teflex sheet. Continue dehydrating for 10 – 12 hours, or until desired crispness is obtained.

Flax Crackers

4 C   whole flaxseeds, soaked 4 – 6 hours in 3 C water

⅓– ½ C Bragg Liquid Aminos (depends on desired saltiness)

juice of 2 – 3 lemons

Mix flax seeds, Bragg and lemon juice; adjust seasonings. Be sure to keep the mixture moist and loose for spreading. Spread mixture as thin as possible (approximately ¼″ thick) on dehydrator trays with teflex sheets. Keeping hands wet will help in the spreading of the flax seeds. Dehydrate at 105° for 5 – 6 hours, flip crackers over and remove the teflex sheet. Continue dehydrating for 4 – 5 hours, or until the mixture is completely dry. For variety add garlic, onions, carrot juice, taco seasoning, Italian seasoning, chili powder, or cumin in any combination. Be creative and make up your own recipe!

Crackers

Mexican Flax Crackers

6 C   flaxseeds, soaked 4 – 6 hours in 5½ C water

4   medium tomatoes, blended

1   red bell pepper, finely chopped

1   red onion, blended

½ C   Bragg Liquid Aminos

2 T   lemon juice

2 t   chili powder

2 t   dried cilantro

1 t   garlic powder

Mix all ingredients well and adjust seasonings. Be sure to keep the mixture moist and loose for spreading. Spread mixture as thin as possible (approximately ¼″ thick) on dehydrator trays with teflex sheets. Keeping hands wet will help in the spreading of the flax seeds. Dehydrate at 105° for 5 – 6 hours, flip crackers over, and remove the teflex sheet. Continue dehydrating for 4 – 5 hours, or until the mixture is completely dry.

Oat Flax Crackers

(Recipe by Elaine Nigro)

4 C   oat groats, soaked 48 hours

1 C   flaxseeds, soaked 4 hours

1/2   onion

3 – 5 cloves garlic

1/4 C lemon juice

6 T   Bragg Liquid Aminos

Process all ingredients in a food processor using the "s" blade until oats become creamy and smooth (approximately 10 minutes) Spread mixture as thin as possible using a rubber spatula (approximately 1/4″ thick) on dehydrator trays with a teflex sheet. Dehydrate at 105° for 2 – 4 hours, flip crackers over and remove teflex sheet. Continue dehydrating for 2 – 4 hours, or until the mixture is completely dry.

Sunny Flax Crackers

2 C   sunflower seeds, soaked 6 hours and rinsed

1   red onion

2 C   flaxseeds, soaked 4 – 6 hours in 1$\frac{1}{3}$ C water

$\frac{1}{4}$ C   Bragg Liquid Aminos

1 T   dried basil

1 T   dried oregano

1 T   dried thyme

Process sunflower seeds and onions through a Champion Juicer using the solid plate. Add flax seeds, Bragg, basil, oregano, and thyme; mix well. Spread mixture 1/4″ thick on a dehydrator tray with a teflex sheet. Keeping hands wet will help in the spreading of the flax seeds. Dehydrate at 105° for 5 – 6 hours, flip the crackers over, and remove the teflex sheet. Score the crackers into small squares with a knife. Continue dehydrating for 5 – 6 hours, or until the mixture is completely dry.

Rye Crackers

2 C   rye, sprouted 2 days

2 C   soft wheat, sprouted 1 day

1/4 C honey dates

1   small yellow onion, cut into large chunks

2 T   raw tahini

2 T   Bragg Liquid Aminos

1 T   caraway seeds

Process rye, wheat, dates, and onion through a Champion Juicer using the solid plate or a food processor using the "s" blade. Add tahini, Bragg, and caraway seeds; mix well. Spread the mixture 1/4˝ thick on a dehydrator tray with a teflex sheet. Dehydrate at 105° for 2 hours, and then score with a knife into squares. Continue dehydrating for 2 hours, flip crackers over, and remove teflex sheet. Continue dehydrating for approximately 4 hours, or until desired moisture is obtained.

Crackers

Rye Crisps

4 C   rye, sprouted 2 days

1   medium yellow onion

2 T   Bragg Liquid Aminos

1 T   caraway seeds

Process rye and onions through a Champion Juicer using the solid plate or a food processor using the "s" blade. Add Bragg and caraway seeds; mix well. Spread mixture very thin (approximately 1/8″ – 1/4″ thick) on a dehydrator tray with a teflex sheet. Dehydrate at 105° for 2 hours, and then score with a knife into squares. Continue dehydrating for 2 hours, flip crackers over, and remove teflex sheet. Continue dehydrating for approximately 2 – 4 hours, or until desired moisture is obtained. These should be fairly dry to resemble Rye Krisps.

Sesame Crackers

1 C   sunflower seeds, soaked 6 hours and rinsed

1 C   sesame seeds, soaked 6 hours

1 C   carrot pulp

1   small red onion

2 T   lemon juice

1 T   Bragg Liquid Aminos

1 t   cumin

1 t   curry

Process all ingredients (use only 1/2 C sesame seeds, saving the rest for topping) until smooth in a food processor using the "s" blade. Form into balls using 2 teaspoons of batter, and sprinkle with remaining sesame seeds. Place on a dehydrator tray with a teflex sheet and flatten to 1/4". Dehydrate at 105° for 2 hours, flip crackers over, and remove teflex sheet. Continue dehydrating for 4 hours, or until desired crispness is obtained.

Crackers

Sunny Vegetable Crackers

2 C   sunflower seeds, soaked 6 – 8 hours and rinsed

2   ears corn

1   tomato

2   stalks celery

1   red bell pepper

1   zucchini

1/2 C red onion

2   cloves garlic

1/2 C fresh parsley

2 t   Bragg Liquid Aminos

Process sunflower seeds, corn, tomato, celery, red bell pepper, zucchini, red onion, garlic, and parsley through a Champion Juicer using the solid plate. Add Bragg and mix well. Form mixture into 2″ round crackers approximately 1/4″ thick. Place on a dehydrator tray with a teflex sheet. Dehydrate at 105° for 4 hours, flip crackers over, and remove teflex sheet. Continue dehydrating for 4 – 6 hours, or until desired crispness is obtained.

Vegetable Crackers

1 C   sunflower seeds, soaked 6 – 8 hours and rinsed

1 C   pumpkin seeds, soaked 6 – 8 hours

2   carrots

1   red bell pepper, finely chopped

1   red onion, finely chopped

2   stalks celery, finely chopped

2   cloves garlic (optional)

¼ C   fresh parsley, finely chopped

1 T   Bragg Liquid Aminos

Process sunflower seeds, pumpkin seeds, and carrots through a Champion Juicer using the solid plate. Add red bell peppers, red onion, celery, garlic, parsley, and Bragg. Form round crackers about 1½″ in diameter and ¼″ thick. Place on a dehydrator tray with a teflex sheet. Dehydrate at 105° for 4 hours, flip crackers over, and remove teflex sheet. Continue dehydrating for 3 – 6 hours, or until desired crispness is obtained.

Crackers

Desserts

Banana Nut Cream Torte
(Recipe by Colleen Holland)

Torte (first and third layer):

2 C pecans, soaked for 6 hours and then dehydrated for 8 hours (this makes the cake more creamy)

1½ C dehydrated bananas, chopped

3/4 C raisins

1 t vanilla

1 t cinnamon

Process pecans, dried bananas, and raisins through a Champion Juicer using the solid plate or a food processor using the "s" blade. Add vanilla and cinnamon; mix well. Divide dough into two sections, and form into desired shape; set aside. If the dough is too soft or warm, refrigerate while you are making the cream and icing.

Cream filling (second layer):

1 ripe banana

3/4 C honey dates, soaked 1 hour (discard soaking water)

1 t vanilla

Continued on next page

Cakes

Banana Nut Cream Torte

Continued

Process all ingredients through a Champion Juicer using the solid plate, or a food processor using the "s" blade. Using the cream filling, ice the first cake layer and place second layer on top.

Frosting:

2 C   dates, soaked 1 hour (discard soak water)

1 C   pine nuts, soaked 1 hour

1 t   vanilla

Process ingredients through a Champion Juicer using the solid plate or in a food processor using the "s" blade. Ice the top and sides of cake. Garnish with chopped pecans or sliced bananas. Refrigerate cake 1 – 2 hours before serving.

Carrot Cake

6 C   carrots

1½ C almonds, soaked 12 – 48 hours and blanched

1½ C honey dates

1 C   shredded coconut

1½ C raisins

1 C   walnuts, soaked 6 – 8 hours and chopped

2 T   psyllium powder

1½ t vanilla

½ t   cinnamon

Process carrots, almonds, and dates through a Champion Juicer using the solid plate. Add coconut, raisins, walnuts, psyllium, vanilla, and cinnamon; mix well. Press dough into dish or pan, making sure to press firmly to compact the mixture. Refrigerate about 1 hour before icing the cake.

Continued on next page

Cakes

Carrot Cake

Continued

Icing:

- 2 C   honey dates
- 1 C   pine nuts
- 2 T   lemon juice
- 1 t   vanilla
- 1 t   lemon zest

Blend dates, pine nuts, lemon juice, vanilla, and lemon zest in food processor using the "s" blade or in a blender until smooth; add a little water if necessary. Refrigerate 1 – 2 hours before icing the cake. Garnish with chopped walnuts if desired.

David's Cake

1 C   almonds, soaked 12 – 48 hours and blanched

1 C   raisins

1/2 C mission figs

1/2 C pecans, soaked 6 hours

4   dehydrated bananas

1 t   vanilla

Process almonds, raisins, figs, pecans, and bananas through a Champion Juicer using the solid plate to form the dough. Add vanilla and mix well. Refrigerate the dough for about one hour and then form into desired shape (round, oval, or square).

Icing:

1 C   honey dates

1/2 C walnuts, soaked 6 hours

1/4 C raw carob powder

1 t   vanilla

Process dates, walnuts, and carob powder in a food processor using the "s" blade. Add vanilla and mix well. Ice the sides and top of cake with a knife.

Cakes

Divine Strawberry Torte Cake

First layer:

2 C   almonds, soaked 12 – 48 hours and blanched

2 C   honey dates

6   dehydrated bananas

1 t   vanilla

1 t   cinnamon

Process all ingredients through a Champion Juicer using the solid plate or a food processor using the "s" blade. If the dough is too warm and soft, place it in refrigerator for 1/2 hour. Form dough into a rectangular shape.

Filling:

1 C   strawberries, thinly sliced

Place sliced strawberries on top of first layer in rows.

Continued on next page

Divine Strawberry Torte Cake
Continued

Second layer:

   2 C   Brazil nuts, soaked 6 hours

   2 C   raisins

Process Brazil nuts and raisins through a Champion Juicer using the solid plate, or in a food processor using the "s" blade. Form dough into a rectangular shape the same size as the first layer, and carefully place on top.

Topping:

   1 C   hazelnuts, soaked and finely chopped

   1 C   strawberries, thinly sliced

Press hazelnuts on the sides of cake, and arrange strawberries in rows on top of cake in an attractive manner.

Cakes

Lemon Nut Torte

(Recipe by Richard Salome)

First layer:

  2 C   Brazil nuts, soaked 12 hours

  2 C   raisins

Process Brazil nuts and raisins in a food processor using the "s" blade. Form mixture into desired shape.

Filling and icing:

  3/4 C honey dates

  1/4 C lemon juice

  1 T   lemon zest

Process dates, lemon juice, and zest in a food processor using the "s" blade until smooth. Use half for filling, and save the remainder to ice the second layer.

Continued on next page

Lemon Nut Torte

Continued

Second layer:

2 C   almonds, soaked 12 – 48 hours and blanched

2 C   raisins

Process almonds and raisins in a food processor using the "s" blade. Form into the same shape as the first layer. Place second layer on top of first. Use remaining lemon-date icing to frost top of cake.

Optional:

1 C   hazelnuts, soaked 6 – 8 hours and finely chopped

Press nuts on the sides of the cake.

Cakes

Lover's Cake

2 C   walnuts, soaked 6 – 8 hours and dehydrated 8 hours

4   dehydrated bananas

2 C   honey dates

2 T   raw carob powder

1 t   vanilla

½ C   hazelnuts, soaked 6 – 8 hours, dehydrated 8 hours, and
       chopped

Process walnuts and dehydrated bananas in a food processor
using the "s" blade. Slowly add dates to the mixture. Add carob,
vanilla; mix well. Form dough into desired shape. Press chopped
hazelnuts around the outside of the cake. Refrigerate for 1 – 2
hours before serving.

Starlight Coconut Cake

*(Created for Pam Masters by Colleen Holland and
Rose Lee Calabro)*

Colleen and I created this cake to express our eternal love and gratitude to Pam Masters. We made it into a three-tiered, wedding-style cake covered with fresh pink and white roses. The cake served over 125 people who attended Pam's raw living food party in April, 1998.

1 C	almonds, soaked 12 – 48 hours and dehydrated 10 hours
1 C	pecans, soaked 6 hours and dehydrated 6 hours
5	dehydrated bananas
3 C	medjool dates
3/4 t	coconut extract
1/2 t	vanilla

Process almonds and pecans in a food processor using the "s" blade until nuts are finely chopped. Slowly add the dehydrated bananas, dates, coconut extract, and vanilla. Continue processing until the dough has a smooth texture. Mold dough into desired shape.

Continued on next page

Starlight Coconut Cake

Continued

Icing:

2 C   medjool dates, soaked 1 hour (save water)

1 C   pine nuts

6 T   soak water from dates

2 t   vanilla

½ C   shredded coconut

Process dates, pine nuts, and vanilla in a food processor using the "s" blade until smooth and creamy; add date soak water for consistency if necessary. Spread icing on cake, and press shredded coconut into top and sides of cake.

Strawberry Cheesecake

2 C almonds, soaked 12 – 48 hours and blanched

1 C pine nuts, soaked 2 hours

1 C shredded coconut, soaked 2 hours

½ C medjool dates (add more if you want the cheesecake to be sweeter)

2–4 T psyllium powder

1 t vanilla

Topping:

2 C fresh strawberries

Process almonds, pine nuts, coconut, and dates through a Champion Juicer using the solid plate; mix well. Add psyllium powder and vanilla, adjusting psyllium according to consistency desired. Put mixture in a 8˝ springform pan, and refrigerate 2 hours. In a blender, or food processor with the "s" blade, process strawberries until they are chunky. Remove cheesecake from springform pan and spread topping over the cake.

Strawberry Mousse
Pinwheel Cake

Cake:

3 C   pecans, soaked 6 – 8 hours and dehydrated 8 hours

2 C   honey dates

1 t   cardamom

1 t   vanilla

Mousse:

1 C   pine nuts

20   strawberries

1½ C honey dates

1 t   vanilla

Process pecans in a food processor using the "s" blade until creamy and smooth. Spread the mousse evenly on cake. Roll cake into a cylinder, cover and place in a refrigerator for several hours. After refrigeration, roll pinwheel cake in soaked chopped nuts or shredded coconut before slicing.

Triple Berry Bars

(Recipe by Colleen Holland)

Crust:

2 C   almonds, soaked 12 – 48 hours and blanched

1 C   medjool dates

1 t   cinnamon

1 t   vanilla

Process almonds, dates, vanilla, and cinnamon in a food processor using the "s" blade. Press into 9″ x 12″ pan.

Filling:

4 C   chopped berries (strawberries, raspberries, blueberries, or boysenberries)

1 C   honey dates

1/3 C   apple juice

1 t   vanilla

1/4 t   cinnamon

6 T   psyllium husk powder

Continued on next page

Triple Berry Bars

Continued

Purée 2 cups of berries with dates, apple juice, vanilla, cinnamon, and psyllium husk powder in a food processor using the "s" blade. Pour remaining 2 cups of chopped berries onto crust, and pour purée mixture over it.

Creme frosting:

    1 C   walnuts, soaked 6 – 8 hours and dehydrated 8 hours

    ½ C dates, soaked (save soak water)

    1 t   vanilla

Process walnuts in a food processor using the "s" blade, until creamy. Add dates, a small amount of soak water, and vanilla until smooth. Frost bars after crust and filling have been refrigerated for several hours. Cut into squares, and garnish with fresh berries and mint leaves.

Apricot Truffles

1 C   almonds, soaked 12 – 48 hours and blanched

1 C   dried apricots

½ C   honey dates

1 T   lemon zest

1 t   vanilla

Process almonds, apricots, and dates through a Champion Juicer using the solid plate or a food processor using the "s" blade. Add lemon zest and vanilla. Form dough into small balls and chill before serving.

Hazelnut Log

2 C   hazelnuts, soaked 6 – 8 hours and chopped

1 C   black mission figs, soaked 1 hour

1/2 C dates, soaked 1 hour

1/4 C raw carob powder

1/4 C water (approx.)

1 C   sesame seeds, soaked 6 – 8 hours

1 C   shredded coconut

Process hazelnuts, figs, dates, carob, and water in a food processor using the "s" blade. Add sesame seeds and mix well. Form into a log and roll in shredded coconut. Refrigerate for 2 hours and then slice.

Heavenly Carob Truffle

½ C almonds, soaked 12 – 48 hours and dehydrated 8 hours

½ C pecans, soaked 6 – 8 hours and dehydrated 8 hours

½ C pine nuts

1 C medjool dates

2 T raw carob powder

1 t vanilla

1 C shredded coconut

Process almonds, pecans, and pine nuts in a food processor using the "s" blade. Slowly add dates, and continue processing until the mixture forms a ball. Add carob and vanilla; mix well. Form mixture into 1/2″ balls and roll in coconut. Refrigerate for 2 hours and serve.

Candy

Ice Candy

1 C almonds, soaked 12 – 48 hours and blanched

2 bananas

4 medjool dates, soaked in 1/4 C water

1 Fuji apple

½ C shredded coconut

1 t cinnamon

1 t vanilla

Process almonds, bananas, dates, apple, and coconut through a Champion Juicer using the solid plate or a food processor using the "s" blade. Add cinnamon, date soak water, and vanilla; mix well. Spread in an 8″ glass pan and place in freezer. Cut into pieces and eat frozen. This is delicious served with Decadent Fudge Brownies.

Raisin Balls

2 C raisins

2 C sesame seeds, soaked 6 hours

Process raisins through a Champion Juicer using the solid plate; add sesame seeds and mix well. Roll dough into balls and refrigerate. You can roll the balls in raw carob powder, coconut or some chopped nuts.

Snow Drops

2 C   sunflower seeds, soaked 6 – 8 hours and rinsed

1/2 C honey dates

1/2 C raisins

2 T   flax oil

2 T   raw tahini

1 t   cinnamon

1 t   vanilla

1 C   walnuts, soaked 6 hours and finely chopped

1 C   shredded coconut

Process sunflower seeds, dates, and raisins through a Champion Juicer using the solid plate. Add flax oil, raw tahini, cinnamon, vanilla, and nuts; mix well. Form dough into balls, and roll in coconut. Refrigerate in an air-tight container and store in refrigerator.

Turtles

(Recipe by Colleen Holland)

2³/₄ C raw wild honey

2 t   cinnamon

1 t   vanilla

1¹/₂ C walnuts, soaked 6 – 8 hours

1¹/₂ C pecans, soaked 6 – 8 hours

In a large bowl, mix honey, cinnamon, and vanilla until a smooth paste is formed. Stir in walnuts and pecans, thoroughly coating. Form into small clusters on a dehydrator tray with a teflex sheet and dehydrate at 105° for 12 hours. Remove teflex sheet, and continue dehydrating for at least 12 hours.

Candy

Almond Cookies

2 C   almonds, soaked 12 – 48 hours and blanched

1   banana

1 C   dates, soaked 1 hour (discard soak water)

½ C   coconut

1 t   almond extract

18   almonds for garnish, soaked 12 – 48 hours and blanched

Process 2 cups almonds, banana, and dates through a Champion Juicer using the solid plate or a food processor using the "s" blade. Add coconut and almond extract; mix well. Spoon 1 heaping teaspoon dough onto a teflex sheet on a dehydrator tray, and flatten dough into a round approximately 2″ across and 1/4″ thick. Press half of an almond into the middle of each cookie and dehydrate at 105° for 4 hours. Turn cookies over, and remove teflex sheet. Continue dehydrating for 3 – 4 hours, or until desired moisture is obtained.

Almond Orange Cookies

2 C   almonds, soaked 12 – 48 hours and blanched

2 C   sunflower seeds, soaked 6 – 8 hours and rinsed

2   bananas

1½ C honey dates

2 t   almond extract

1 C   shredded coconut

⅓ C fresh orange peel

Process almonds, sunflower seeds, bananas, and dates through a Champion Juicer using the solid plate. Add almond extract; mix well. Using a food processor with the "s" blade, blend the coconut and orange peel. Form dough into small balls, and roll in the coconut and orange peel mixture. Place on a dehydrator tray with a teflex sheet and flatten cookies to ½″. Place cookies close together on the sheets. Dehydrate at 105° for 4 hours, turn cookies over and remove teflex sheet. Continue dehydrating for 3 – 5 hours, or until desired moisture is obtained.

Cookies

Apple Raisin Cookies

2 C sunflower seeds, soaked 6 – 8 hours and rinsed

2 Fuji apples

2 large bananas

1/2 C honey dates

1 t vanilla

1 t cinnamon

1 C raisins

1 C walnuts, soaked 6 – 8 hours and chopped

Process sunflower seeds, apples, bananas, and dates through a Champion Juicer using the solid plate. In a large bowl, mix dough with vanilla, cinnamon, raisins, and walnuts. Spoon dough on a dehydrator tray with a teflex sheet, and form into small round cookies. Dehydrate at 105° for 4 – 6 hours, turn cookies over and remove teflex sheet. Continue dehydrating for 4 – 6 hours, or until desired moisture is obtained.

Apricot Cookies

2 C   sunflower seeds, soaked 6 – 8 hours and rinsed

1 C   dried apricots, soaked, or 2 C fresh

½ C honey dates

1   banana

1 t   vanilla

1 t   cardamom

1 C   hazelnuts, pecans, or walnuts, soaked 6 – 8 hours
       and finely chopped

Process sunflower seeds, apricots, dates, and banana through a
Champion Juicer using the solid plate. In a large bowl, mix dough
with vanilla, cardamom, and nuts. Spoon dough on a dehydrator
tray with a teflex sheet, and form into small round cookies.
Dehydrate at 105° for 4 – 6 hours, turn cookies over, and remove
teflex sheet. Continue dehydrating for 4 – 6 hours, or until desired
moisture is obtained.

Banana Cookies

2 C   barley, soaked 2 days

3   bananas

2   persimmons

1/2 C honey dates

1 C   water

1 t   vanilla

1 t   cinnamon

1 C   walnuts, soaked 6 – 8 hours and chopped

1 C   raisins

Place barley, bananas, persimmons, dates, water, vanilla, and cinnamon in a blender; mix until thick and smooth. Add chopped walnuts and raisins; mix well. Spoon dough on a dehydrator tray with a teflex sheet, and form into small round cookies. Dehydrate at 105° for 4 – 6 hours, turn cookies over, and remove teflex sheet. Continue dehydrating for 4 – 6 hours, or until desired moisture is obtained.

Banana Nut Cookies

2 C   sunflower seeds, soaked 6 – 8 hours and rinsed

1 C   almonds, soaked 12 – 48 hours and blanched

4   bananas

½ C   honey dates

1 t   vanilla

1 t   cinnamon

1 C   walnuts, soaked 6 – 8 hours and finely chopped

Process sunflower seeds, almonds, bananas, and dates through a Champion Juicer using the solid plate. In a large bowl, mix dough with vanilla, cinnamon, and walnuts. Spoon dough on a dehydrator tray with a teflex sheet, and form into small round cookies. Dehydrate at 105° for 4 – 6 hours, turn cookies over, and remove teflex sheet. Continue dehydrating for 4 – 6 hours, or until desired moisture is obtained.

Brendan's High Energy Bars

1 C   barley, soaked 2 days

2 C   soft wheat berries, sprouted 1 day

¾ C   honey dates

3 T   raw honey

1 t   vanilla

1 t   cinnamon

1 C   walnuts, soaked 6 – 8 hours and chopped

½ C   almonds, soaked 12 – 48 hours, blanched and chopped

Process barley, wheat, and dates through a Champion Juicer using the solid plate. Add honey, vanilla, cinnamon, walnuts, and almonds; mix well. Form into bars, and place on dehydrator tray with a teflex sheet. Dehydrate at 105° for 4 hours, turn bars over, and remove teflex sheets. Continue dehydrating for 4 – 6 hours, or until desired moisture is obtained.

Carob Mint Cookies

2 C   almonds, soaked 12 – 48 hours and blanched

2 C   sunflower seeds, soaked 6 – 8 hours and rinsed

2 C   honey dates

1 C   raisins

1 C   raw carob powder

2 t   vanilla

1 C   shredded coconut

1   bunch of fresh mint (leaves only)

Process almonds, sunflower seeds, dates, and raisins through a Champion Juicer using the solid plate. Add carob powder and vanilla; mix well. Using a food processor with the "s" blade, process coconut and fresh mint. Form dough into small balls, and roll in coconut mint mixture to coat. Place on a dehydrator tray with a teflex sheet, and flatten into smooth round cookies ³/₈″ thick. Dehydrate at 105° for 4 hours, turn cookies over, and remove teflex sheet. Continue dehydrating for 4 – 6 hours, or until desired moisture is obtained.

Carrot Cookies

1½ C   barley, soaked 2 days

4   large carrots, finely grated

1   medium banana

1 C   water

2 C   raisins

1 C   water

1 t   cinnamon

1 t   vanilla

¼ t   fresh grated nutmeg

1 C   walnuts, soaked 6 – 8 hours and chopped

Place barley, carrots, banana, water, and 1 cup of raisins in a blender; blend until mixture is thick and smooth. Add cinnamon, vanilla, nutmeg, walnuts and the remaining cup of raisins to mixture; mix well. Spoon dough on a dehydrator tray with a teflex sheet, and form into small round cookies. Dehydrate at 105° for 4 – 6 hours, turn cookies over, and remove teflex sheet. Continue dehydrating for 4 – 6 hours, or until desired moisture is obtained.

Chunky Apple Cookies

2 C   barley, soaked 2 days

1 C   water

1 C   honey dates

2   large apples, chopped

1 t   vanilla

1 t   cinnamon

1 C   walnuts, soaked 6 hours and chopped

1 C   raisins

Place barley, water, dates, apples, vanilla, and cinnamon in a blender; mix until thick and smooth. Add chopped walnuts and raisins; mix well. Spoon dough on a dehydrator tray with a teflex sheet, and form into small round cookies. Dehydrate at 105° for 4 – 6 hours, turn cookies over, and remove teflex sheet. Continue dehydrating for 4 – 6 hours, or until desired moisture is obtained.

Cookies

Claudia's Cookies

2 C almonds, soaked 12 – 48 hours and blanched

2 C sunflower seeds, soaked 6 – 8 hours and rinsed

1 C honey dates

½ C dried apricots, soaked 4 hours

1 t vanilla

1 t cinnamon

1 t cardamom

2 C pecans, soaked 6 – 8 hours and chopped

Process almonds, sunflower seeds, dates, and apricots through the Champion Juicer using the solid plate. Add vanilla, cinnamon, and cardamom; mix well. Form dough into small balls, and roll in the chopped pecans. Place on a dehydrator tray with a teflex sheet, and form into small round cookies. Dehydrate at 105° for 4 hours, turn cookies over, and remove teflex sheet. Continue dehydrating for 4 – 6 hours, or until desired moisture is obtained.

Decadent Fudge Brownies

2 C sunflower seeds, soaked 6 – 8 hours and rinsed

1 C pine nuts, soaked 2 hours

1 C honey dates

1 banana

1/4 C carob

1 t vanilla

1 T maple syrup

1 C walnuts, soaked 6 – 8 hours and chopped

Process sunflower seeds, pine nuts, dates, and banana through a Champion Juicer using the solid plate or a food processor using the "s" blade. Add carob, vanilla, maple syrup, and walnuts; mix well. Form dough into desired shape approximately 1/2″ thick using 1/4 C of dough for each brownie. Place on a dehydrator tray with a teflex sheet. Dehydrate at 105° for 4 hours, turn brownies over, and remove teflex sheet. Continue dehydrating for 4 – 6 hours, or until desired moisture is obtained.

Continued on next page

Cookies

Decadent Fudge Brownies
Continued

Icing (optional):

1/4 C   maple syrup

1 t   vanilla

1/4 C   raw carob powder

Mix maple syrup and vanilla in a small bowl until creamy. Add carob a little at a time; mix well. Let icing sit for about 30 minutes, then spread brownies with a thin layer of icing. This icing is very rich but delicious.

Island Fantasy Cookies

1½ C barley, soaked 2 days

½ C honey dates

⅓ C water

1 orange, peeled

1 t orange zest

1 t vanilla

1 C shredded coconut

½ C raisins

2 T carob powder

1 C walnuts, soaked 6 – 8 hours and chopped

Place barley, dates, water, and orange in a blender; blend until mixture is thick and smooth. Add zest, vanilla, coconut, raisins, carob, and walnuts; mix well. Spoon dough on a dehydrator tray with a teflex sheet, and form into small round cookies. Dehydrate at 105° for 4 – 6 hours, turn cookies over, and remove teflex sheet. Continue dehydrating for 4 – 6 hours, or until desired moisture is obtained.

Oatmeal Raisin Cookies

2 C   oat groats, sprouted 2 days

1 C   barley, soaked 2 days

¾ C   honey dates

1 C   water

1   banana

1 t   vanilla

1 t   cinnamon

1 C   walnuts, soaked 6 – 8 hours and chopped

1 C   raisins

Process oats, barley, dates, water, and banana in a blender until mixture is smooth and thick. Add the vanilla and cinnamon; blend again. Stir in the walnuts and raisins. Spoon dough on a dehydrator tray with a teflex sheet, and form into small round cookies. Dehydrate at 105° for 4 – 6 hours, turn cookies over, and remove teflex sheet. Continue dehydrating for 4 – 6 hours, or until desired moisture is obtained.

Persimmon Cookies

1½ C barley, soaked 2 days

1 C   water

2   large persimmons

1 C   honey dates

1 t   cinnamon

1 C   walnuts, chopped

1 C   raisins

Process barley, water, persimmons, dates, and cinnamon in a blender until mixture is smooth and thick. Add walnuts and raisins; mix well. Spoon dough on a dehydrator tray with a teflex sheet and form into small round cookies. Dehydrate at 105° for 4 – 6 hours, turn cookies over, and remove teflex sheet. Continue dehydrating for 4 – 6 hours, or until desired moisture is obtained.

Cookies

Pineapple Apricot Cookies

2 C   sunflower seeds, soaked 6 – 8 hours and rinsed

1 C   almonds, soaked 12 – 48 hours and blanched

½ C   honey dates

3   slices dried pineapple, soaked, or 1 C fresh

¼ C   dried apricots, soaked, or 1 C fresh

1   banana

1 t   vanilla

1 C   hazelnuts, soaked 6 – 8 hours and chopped

Process sunflower seeds, almonds, dates, pineapple, apricots and banana through a Champion Juicer using the solid plate. Add vanilla and hazelnuts; mix well. Spoon dough on a dehydrator tray with a teflex sheet, and form into small round cookies. Dehydrate at 105° for 4 – 6 hours, turn cookies over, and remove teflex sheet. Continue dehydrating for 4 – 6 hours, or until desired moisture is obtained.

Strawberry Cookies

2 C   sunflower seeds, soaked 6 – 8 hours and rinsed

1 C   almonds, soaked 12 – 48 hours and blanched

1 C   dried strawberries, soaked 2 hours, or 2 C fresh

2   bananas

½ C   honey dates

1 t   vanilla

1 C   walnuts soaked 6 – 8 hours and finely chopped

Process sunflower seeds, almonds, strawberries, bananas, and dates through a Champion Juicer using the solid plate. Add vanilla and walnuts; mix well. Spoon dough on a dehydrator tray with a teflex sheet, and form into small round cookies. Dehydrate at 105° for 4 – 6 hours, turn cookies over, and remove teflex sheet. Continue dehydrating for 4 – 6 hours, or until desired moisture is obtained.

Strawberry Banana Cookies

1½ C barley, soaked 2 days

¾ C honey dates

½ C water

3 bananas

½ C fresh strawberries

1 t vanilla

1 C walnuts, soaked 6 hours and chopped

Process barley, dates, water, bananas, strawberries, and vanilla in a blender until mixture is thick and smooth. Add chopped walnuts; mix well. Spoon dough on a dehydrator tray with a teflex sheet and form into small round cookies. Dehydrate at 105° for 4 – 6 hours, turn cookies over, and remove teflex sheet. Continue dehydrating for 4 – 6 hours, or until desired moisture is obtained.

Tropical Cookies

2 C   sunflower seeds, soaked 6 – 8 hours and rinsed

1 C   almonds, soaked 12 – 48 hours and blanched

1 C   fresh pineapple, or 1/2 C dried, soaked

1 C   fresh mango, or 1/2 C dried, soaked

2   bananas

1/2 C honey dates

1 t   vanilla

1 C   pecans, soaked 6 – 8 hours and finely chopped

Process sunflower seeds, almonds, pineapple, mango, bananas, and dates through a Champion Juicer using the solid plate. Add vanilla and pecans; mix well. Spoon dough on a dehydrator tray with a teflex sheet and form into small round cookies. Dehydrate at 105° for 4 – 6 hours, turn cookies over, and remove teflex sheet. Continue dehydrating for 4 – 6 hours, or until desired moisture is obtained.

Banana Ice Cream

4   frozen bananas

Run frozen bananas through a Champion Juicer using the solid plate to make this delicious ice cream. Serve immediately.

Banana Persimmon Ice Cream

2   frozen persimmons
3   frozen bananas

Alternate frozen persimmons and bananas through a Champion Juicer using the solid plate. Serve immediately.

Blueberry Ice Cream

1 C   frozen blueberries

6   frozen bananas

Alternate frozen bananas and blueberries through a Champion Juicer using the solid plate. Serve immediately.

Carob Ice Cream

2 T   raw carob powder

1 T   warm water

6   large frozen bananas

6   honey dates

1/4 C walnuts, soaked 6 – 8 hours, chopped

Mix carob powder with warm water until smooth. Alternate frozen bananas and dates through the Champion Juicer using the solid plate. Stir in carob mixture and sprinkle with walnuts. Serve immediately.

Carob Mint Ice Cream

2 T   raw carob powder

1 T   warm water

6   large frozen bananas

4   dates

1/8 t   peppermint extract

1/4 C pecans, soaked, chopped

      fresh mint leaves

Mix carob powder with warm water until smooth. Alternate frozen bananas and dates through the Champion Juicer using the solid plate. Stir in carob mixture and peppermint extract. Sprinkle with pecans and garnish with fresh mint leaves. Serve immediately.

Honeydew Sorbet

1   large frozen honeydew melon

Process frozen honeydew melon through a Champion Juicer using the solid plate. Serve immediately.

Orange Sherbet

frozen peeled oranges

Process frozen oranges through a Champion Juicer using the solid plate to make this delicious orange sherbet ice cream. Serve immediately.

Ice Creams

Pineapple Surprise Sorbet

1   frozen pineapple, peeled and diced

Process frozen pineapple through a Champion Juicer using the solid plate. Serve immediately.

Optional:

Add a frozen orange or frozen strawberries.

Strawberry Ice Cream

1 C   frozen strawberries
4   large frozen bananas

Alternate frozen strawberries and bananas through a Champion Juicer using the solid plate. Serve immediately.

Triple Berry Ice Cream

4   large frozen bananas

1 C   frozen strawberries

1/2 C   frozen raspberries

1/2 C   frozen blackberries

Alternate frozen bananas, strawberries, raspberries, and blackberries through a Champion Juicer using the solid plate. Serve immediately.

Tropical Delight

4   frozen bananas

1 C   frozen mango

1 C   frozen papaya

Alternate frozen bananas, mango and papaya through a Champion Juicer using the solid plate. Serve immediately.

Ice Creams

Tutti Frutti Ice Cream

4	frozen bananas
2	frozen lemon sections
8	slices frozen papaya
8	frozen strawberries
2	slices frozen pineapple
1	frozen orange

Alternate frozen fruit through a Champion Juicer using the solid plate. Serve immediately.

Pineapple Guava
(Feijoa) Sauce

1 lb. ripe pineapple guava

1 C   water

½ C dates

Halve pineapple guava crosswise and scoop out the pulp with a melon baller, avoiding any bright green parts or skin (they taste bitter). In a blender, mix the pineapple guava, water, and dates. Refrigerate and serve over ice cream or freeze and process through the Champion Juicer using the solid plate to make ice cream.

Ice Creams

Carob Fudge Sauce

(Recipe by Pam Masters)

1 T   raw carob powder

½ C   water

½ t   vanilla

⅛ t   cinnamon

1½ t Bragg Liquid Aminos

5   medjool dates

¼   large avocado

In a blender, blend carob powder, water, vanilla, cinnamon and Bragg. While the blender is still running, slowly add dates and avocado, and blend until smooth. Add more water if needed for consistency. This is a delicious sauce over ice cream.

Fudge Sauce

1 C   maple syrup

½ C   raw carob powder

⅓ C   olive oil

1 T   vanilla

Blend all ingredients until smooth.

Apple Pie

Crust:

1 C   almonds, soaked 12 – 48 hours and blanched

1 C   sunflower seeds, soaked 6 – 8 hours

½ C   mission figs

1 t   cinnamon

Process all ingredients in a food processor using the "s" blade until dough forms into a ball. Press dough into a 9" pie plate.

Filling:

4–6   apples (Fujis are my favorite)

1–3 T psyllium

1 t   vanilla

1 t   cinnamon

Process apples, psyllium, vanilla, and cinnamon in a blender. Add more psyllium to adjust the consistency of the filling. Pour into crust and refrigerate until serving. Decorate top of pie with a few slices of thinly sliced apples in the form of a wheel. Add a few sprigs of mint to decorate.

Apple Walnut Pie

Crust:

1 C   almonds, soaked 12 – 48 hours and blanched

1 C   pecans, soaked 6 – 8 hours

¾ C   honey dates

½ t   vanilla

1 t   cinnamon

Process almonds and pecans in a food processor using the "s" blade until finely chopped. Slowly add dates. Add vanilla and cinnamon and mix well. Press dough into a 9" pie plate.

Filling:

4 C   apples, thinly sliced

2 T   lemon juice

1 t   cinnamon

1½ C walnuts, soaked 6 – 8 hours and chopped

Process apples, lemon juice, and cinnamon in a blender until chunky. Sir in walnuts. Pour into crust and refrigerate until serving.

Pies

Berry Pie

Crust:

2 C   almonds, soaked 12 – 48 hours and blanched

½ C dates

1 t   vanilla

Process almonds in a food processor using the "s" blade until finely chopped. Slowly add dates. Add vanilla and mix well. Press dough into a 9" pie plate.

Filling:

4 C   berries, (strawberries, boysenberries, raspberries or any combination)

1 C   apples, finely grated

¼ C dates

4 T   psyllium powder

1 t   vanilla

Process 2 cups of berries, apples, and dates in a food processor using the "s" blade. Add psyllium and vanilla; mix well. Pour mixture into pie crust. Add remaining 2 cups of berries to top of mixture and refrigerate before serving.

Mud Pie

Crust:

1 C   almonds, soaked 12 – 48 hours and blanched

1 C   sunflower seeds, soaked 6 – 8 hours and rinsed

1 C   honey dates

½ C raisins

½ C raw carob powder

1 t   vanilla

Process almonds, sunflower seeds, dates, and raisins through a Champion Juicer using a solid plate or a food processor using the "s" blade. Add carob powder and vanilla; mix well. Press into a 9″ pie plate or tart shell pan.

Filling:

1½ C almonds, soaked 12 – 48 hours and blanched

4   medium bananas

½ C water

1 t   vanilla

Process all ingredients in a blender and pour into pie crust. Place pie in freezer until firm. Decorate with sliced strawberries and fresh mint leaves.

Pies

Pecan Pie

Crust:

- ½ C   almonds, soaked 12 – 48 hours and blanched
- ½ C   walnuts
- 1 C   raisins
- 1 t   cinnamon

Process all ingredients in a food processor using the "s" blade until dough forms into a ball. Press dough into a 9" pie plate.

Filling:

- 1 C   pecans, soaked 6 – 8 hours
- 1 C   dried mission figs, soaked 3 – 4 hours (discard soak water)
- 2   bananas
- ¼ C   honey dates
- 1 t   vanilla
- 1 t   cinnamon
- ¼ t   nutmeg

Process the pecans, figs, bananas, and dates in a food processor using the "s" blade. Add vanilla, cinnamon and nutmeg; mix well. Pour filling into pie crust, decorate with some pecans, and sliced dates. Chill before serving.

Persimmon Pie

Crust:

- ⅓ C sunflower seeds, soaked 6 – 8 hours and rinsed
- ½ C sesame seeds, soaked 6 hours
- ⅓ C almonds, soaked 12 – 48 hours and blanched
- 1 C honey dates

Process all ingredients in a food processor using the "s" blade until dough forms into a ball. Press dough into a 9" pie plate.

Filling:

- 7 medium persimmons
- 3 large medjool dates
- 3 T psyllium powder
- 1 t cinnamon
- ¼ t fresh ground nutmeg
- 1 T shredded coconut

Process persimmons and dates on high speed in a blender until a thick pudding forms. Add psyllium, cinnamon, and nutmeg; mix well. Pour filling into prepared pie crust. Sprinkle with coconut. Chill and serve cold.

Pies

Piña Colada Pie

Crust:

2 C   almonds, soaked 12 – 48 hours and blanched

½ C dates

¼ C mission figs

Process all ingredients in a food processor using the "s" blade until dough forms into a ball. Press dough into a 9" pie plate.

Filling:

4   large bananas

⅓ C shredded coconut

1   small pineapple, cored and peeled

1 t fresh grated nutmeg

2 t raw wild honey

2 T agar-agar

⅓ C water

1   kiwi fruit, peeled and sliced

      shredded coconut

Continued on next page

Piña Colada Pie

Continued

Slice bananas in $1/8''$ diagonals and layer them over pie crust. In a blender, process coconut, pineapple, nutmeg, and honey until smooth. Heat agar-agar with water in a small saucepan over low heat until bubbly and gelatinous, about 3 to 4 minutes. Stirring mixture constantly, add agar-agar mixture to pineapple mixture and blend for 20 seconds. Pour over sliced bananas and allow to cool for several minutes. Place kiwi slices on top of pie in the shape of a fan. Dust with shredded coconut. Chill for several hours before serving.

Pies

Strawberry Banana Pie

Crust:

1 C   almonds, soaked 12 – 48 hours and blanched

1 C   pecans, soaked 6 hours

½ C raisins

½ C honey dates

1 t   cinnamon

Process all ingredients in a food processor using the "s" blade until dough forms into a ball. Press dough into a 9″ pie plate.

Continued on next page

Strawberry Banana Pie
Continued

Filling:

6 C   strawberries

4   honey dates

1–2 T psyllium powder

3   medium bananas

shredded coconut

Process 3 cups strawberries and dates in a food processor using the "s" blade. Add psyllium and mix well. Pour two thirds of the filling into crust, reserving one third for top. Slice the bananas and strawberries as thin as possible on the diagonal. Cover the bottom of the pie crust, with a layer of banana slices and half of the remaining strawberries. Top with a final layer of strawberries and the rest of the filling. Sprinkle with coconut. Refrigerate at least 3 hours before serving.

Pies

Strawberry Pie
(Recipe by Pam Tablak)

Crust:

1 C   almonds, soaked 12 – 48 hours and blanched

½ C   honey dates

Process almonds and honey in a food processor using the "s" blade until dough forms into a ball. Press dough into a 9" pie plate.

Filling:

5 C   strawberries

1 C   almonds, soaked 12 – 48 hours and blanched

1   banana

¼ C   honey dates

Process all ingredients in a Champion Juicer using the solid plate. The filling should be thick, add water for consistency. Pour filling into pie crust and freeze. Garnish with fresh strawberries before serving.

Tastes Like Pumpkin Pie

Filling:

4 C carrots

¾ C almonds, soaked 12 – 48 hours and blanched

½ C walnuts, soaked 6 hours

1½ C honey dates

1 t   vanilla

2 t   cinnamon

1 t   ginger

¼ t   cloves

Process carrots, almonds, walnuts, and dates through a Champion Juicer using the solid plate. Add vanilla, cinnamon, ginger, and cloves; mix well. Press firmly into a 9″ or 10″ pie plate and refrigerate until firm.

Continued on next page

Tastes Like Pumpkin Pie

Continued

Topping:

½ C honey dates

1 C almonds, soaked 12 – 48 hours and blanched

water for consistency

1 t vanilla

1 T shredded coconut

Process dates and almonds through a Champion Juicer using the solid plate. Add vanilla and water; mix well. Using a knife spread topping over filling and sprinkle with coconut. Chill before serving.

Tropical Bliss Pie

(Recipe by Greg LaRoche)

Crust:

2 C	almonds, soaked 12 – 48 hours and blanched
1 C	honey dates
1	orange, peeled
1 t	cinnamon
1/2 t	nutmeg

Process almonds, dates, and orange in a food processor using the "s" blade until a smooth paste is formed. Add cinnamon and nutmeg; mix well. Press crust into a 9" pie plate. Place pie crust in freezer to set for about one hour.

Filling:

4	frozen bananas
2 C	frozen strawberries
1	frozen kiwi

Process frozen bananas, strawberries, and kiwi through a Champion Juicer using the solid plate or in a food processor using the "s" blade. Pour filling into pie crust and decorate top with some fresh fruit.

Pies

Juices

Juicing

Fruit or vegetable juices can help to cleanse the body of toxins. Fruit juices are the cleansers and should be drunk in the morning on an empty stomach. A fruit juice is an excellent way to start the day. Vegetable juices are the toners and builders and should be drunk in the afternoon.

Raw juices contain all the elements of living food, such as enzymes, minerals, and vitamins, in a more concentrated form that is more readily assimilated by the body. Juicing provides alkaline force to the body, which helps to neutralize toxins. Therefore, if a body is depleted of essential vitamins and minerals, juicing is an excellent way to provide the body with dense amounts of nutrients. Raw juices have been used in many healing programs around the world.

A juice meal can easily be prepared in a matter of minutes. This is especially convenient for today's fast-paced lifestyle. The freshness of one's juice is vitally important, so use only fresh and organic produce for juicing.

There are many juicers on the market to match anyone's pocket-book. Juicers are available through department stores, membership stores, mail order, television infomericals, and the Internet. Some of the leading juicers to consider are Norwalk, Champion, Acme, Omega, Juiceman Jr., Juiceman II and Green Power.

Apple Strawberry

2   apples

6   strawberries

Arise and Shine

2   stalks celery

1   cucumber

1   carrot

Citrus Shine

4   tangerines

3   rings fresh pineapple

Cranberry Cocktail

| 3 | apples |
| ½ C | cranberries |

Golden Sunset

6	carrots
6	stalks celery
1	beet
1	lemon
½	cucumber
1″	piece fresh ginger

Green Machine

3	stalks celery
1	cucumber
1	handful spinach
1	carrot

Liver Flush

1   lemon

1   glass of water

This drink is wonderful for cleansing the liver.

Morning Booster

oranges

This makes a wonderful and pure breakfast drink.

Morning Glory

2   oranges

1   grapefruit

1   lemon

Orange Surprise

2   oranges

2   rings fresh pineapple

Pure Apple Bliss

2   apples

2   stalks celery

Skin Sensation

2   carrots

     fresh ginger (optional)

Spring Kicker

1	apple
8	strawberries
2	rings pineapple

Summer Love

2	stalks celery
1	zucchini
1	tomatoes
	handful parsley
1/4 C	basil

Sweet and Innocent

4	carrots
2	apples
1/4	beet

Sweet Sensation

5   carrots

¹/₂   apple

¹/₂″   piece of ginger

Sweetie Pie

red flame grapes

Your children will love this drink. It's very sweet and good for
them.

Tropical Sunrise

2   oranges

¹/₂ C raspberries

3   rings pineapple

Ultimate Energizer

2	stalks celery
1	cucumber
1/2	beet
1	carrot
1/2	lemon

Vegetable Cocktail

2	stalks celery
1	cucumber
1	tomato
1	red bell pepper

Vegetable Heaven

6	carrots
1	apple
2	stalks celery
1/4 C	parsley
1/2	beet

Juices

Veggie Cooler

3   tomatoes

1/2   cucumber

1   stalk celery

1/2   lime

Watermelon Cooler

watermelon

Watermelon tastes delicious on a hot afternoon. It also helps to cleanse the body.

Main Dishes

Carrot Hummus

2 C   garbanzo beans, sprouted

3   green onions, finely chopped

2   carrots, shredded

2   stalks celery, finely chopped

1/2 C raw tahini

1/4 C fresh parsley

2 T   virgin olive oil

1 T   Bragg Liquid Aminos

1 t   dried basil

1 t   dried dill

Process garbanzo beans through a Champion Juicer using the solid plate or a food processor using "s" blade. Add remaining ingredients and mix well.

Main Dishes

Chili

1 C   garbanzo beans, sprouted

1 C   lentils, sprouted

1 C   mung beans, sprouted

1 C   adzuki beans, sprouted

2   carrots, grated

1   stalk celery, finely chopped

1   zucchini, finely chopped

¼ C   flax oil

¼ C   lemon juice

1 T   Bragg Liquid Aminos

2 t   chili powder

      dash of cayenne

Combine all ingredients in a large bowl. Let marinate for 1 hour in the refrigerator before serving.

Cilantro Barley

2 C   barley, soaked 2 days

1 C   fresh cilantro

1   red bell pepper, finely chopped

1 C   celery, finely chopped

1 C   green onions, finely chopped

½ C carrots, finely grated

1 t   cumin

Mix all ingredients in a large bowl.

Dressing:

¼ C lemon juice

2 T   virgin olive oil

2 t   Bragg Liquid Aminos

2   cloves garlic, pressed

Mix all ingredients in a small bowl. Pour over dish and mix well.

Main Dishes

Curried Grain Dish

(Recipe by Richard Salome)

1 C   barley, soaked 2 days

½ C almonds, soaked 12 – 48 hours, blanched and chopped

¼ C sunflower seeds, soaked 6 – 8 hours and rinsed

¼ C flax seed oil

2 T   Spike Salt-Free All Purpose Seasoning

Mix all ingredients in a large bowl.

Sauce:

1 C   almonds, soaked 12 – 48 hours and blanched

1 C   water (approximately)

1   banana

1½ t curry powder

2 T   flax oil

2 T   Bragg Liquid Aminos

2   medium Fuji apples, chopped

1 C   raisins

Continued on next page

Curried Grain Dish

Continued

Process almonds in a blender and add enough water to cover; blend until creamy. Add banana, curry powder, flax oil, and Bragg; continue to process for 20 seconds. Stir in apples and raisins, and pour over the grain dish; stir well. Place dish in a warm location or in a dehydrator for at least 2 hours at 105°.

Main Dishes

Curry Hummus

2 C   garbanzo beans, sprouted

½ C   raw tahini

2   stalks celery, finely chopped

1   carrot, finely grated

1   red onion, finely chopped

1 T   Bragg Liquid Aminos

1 t   cumin

1 t   curry

Process garbanzo beans through a Champion Juicer using the solid plate or a food processor using the "s" blade. Add remaining ingredients and mix well.

Italian Hummus

2 C   garbanzo beans, sprouted

½ C raw tahini

4   green onions, finely chopped

3   stalks celery, finely chopped

¼ C fresh basil, finely chopped

¼ C fresh parsley, finely chopped

2 T   lemon juice

2 T   virgin olive oil

1 T   Bragg Liquid Aminos

Process garbanzo beans through a Champion Juicer using the solid plate or a food processor using the "s" blade. Add remaining ingredients and mix well.

Lasagna

(Recipe by Gail Lanier)

Base:

2 C almonds, soaked 12 – 48 hours and blanched

1½ C sunflower seeds, soaked 6-8 hours and rinsed

3 stalks celery

2 carrots

1 C fresh basil

1 T Bragg Liquid Aminos

1 – 2 cloves garlic

Process all ingredients through a Champion Juicer using the solid plate or a food processor using the "s" blade. In a glass rectangular dish, spread the base and pat lightly.

Continued on next page

Lasagna

Continued

Topping:

    1½ C sun-dried tomatoes, soaked 1 hour (save soak water)

    1 C   fresh basil

    1   clove garlic

Process sun-dried tomatoes in a blender with a little soak water and blend until the consistency of icing. Add basil and garlic; blend to make a spread. Spread topping onto base and garnish with fresh parsley.

Main Dishes

Marinara Sauce

3–4 large peeled tomatoes

4 cloves garlic, minced

2 green onions, chopped

2–3 honey dates

¼ C parsley

3 T virgin olive oil

2 T Italian seasoning

1 T Bragg Liquid Aminos

1–2 t lemon juice

Process tomatoes in a blender for a few seconds. Add remaining ingredients and continue to blend until the sauce is thick and chunky. Serve over prepared vegetable "pasta."

Pasta:

carrot, jicama, sweet potato, yellow squash, and zucchini

Cut vegetables into julienne strips, or use a Cook's Help machine to make fine spaghetti strips.

Marinated Fava Beans

(Adapted from my mother, Ellen Calabro's recipe)

3 C   raw fresh fava beans

½ C   green onions, finely chopped (or red onions or leeks)

½ C   virgin olive oil

4 T   lemon juice

1 T   Bragg Liquid Aminos

2 – 3   cloves garlic, minced

Mix all ingredients in a large bowl and refrigerate for at least 4 – 6 hours. The longer they marinate, the more flavorful the beans. You can eat these as a snack, put them in a salad, or put them on a bed of your favorite sprouts and enjoy.

Mexican Stuffed Peppers

4   Anaheim chilies, rinsed, drained, and seeded

Filling:

1 C   almonds, soaked 12 – 48 hours and blanched

1 C   sunflower seeds, soaked 6 – 8 hours and rinsed

½ C   pumpkin seeds, soaked 6 hours

½ C   lentils, sprouted

½ C   carrots, finely grated

½ C   celery, finely chopped

½ C   cilantro, finely chopped

2 T   lemon juice

1 T   Bragg Liquid Aminos

1 T   chili powder

1 T   cumin

Continued on next page

Process almonds, sunflower seeds, pumpkin seeds, and lentils through a Champion Juicer using the solid plate or a food processor using the "s" blade. In a large bowl, combine processed nuts, seeds, and lentils with remaining ingredients; mix well. Stuff peppers with filling and serve on a bed of sprouts.

Sauce:

2	red bell peppers
2 – 3	dates
1	tomato
1 T	Bragg Liquid Aminos
1 T	carob powder
1 T	lemon juice
½ t	chili powder
	dash of cayenne
	water to blend

Process all ingredients in a blender. Serve on the side with stuffed peppers.

Nut Loaf

1 C   almonds, soaked 12 – 48 hours and blanched

1 C   hazelnuts, soaked 6 – 8 hours

1 C   sunflower seeds, soaked 6 hours and rinsed

1″   piece fresh ginger

4   stalks celery, finely chopped

1   carrot, finely grated

1   red pepper, finely chopped

1   yellow squash, finely chopped

¼ C   parsley, finely chopped

1 T   Bragg Liquid Aminos

1 t   marjoram

½ t   coriander

Process almonds, hazelnuts, sunflower seeds, and ginger through
a Champion Juicer using the solid plate or a food processor using
the "s" blade. Add remaining ingredients and mix well. Form into
a nut loaf and refrigerate for 1 hour. Serve on a bed of your
favorite sprouts.

Oat Burgers

2 C   oat groats, sprouted 2 days

1 C   sunflower seeds, soaked 6 – 8 hours and rinsed

2   carrots, finely grated

2   stalks celery, finely chopped

1   clove garlic, finely minced

2 T   lemon juice

1 T   Bragg Liquid Aminos

2 t   flax oil

1 t   oregano

Process oat groats and sunflower seeds through a Champion Juicer using the solid plate. Add remaining ingredients and mix well. Form into patties and refrigerate for 1 hour. Serve on a bed of sprouts with slices of avocado.

Pasta Mexicana

1½ C tomatoes, diced

1 C fresh corn

1 C cucumbers, julienned

1 C jicama, julienned

1   medium avocado, thinly sliced crosswise

1 C salsa (see recipe)

1 T virgin olive oil

½ t dried oregano

¼ t ground cumin

¼ t chili powder

   dash of cayenne

¼ C cilantro, minced

Combine tomatoes, corn, cucumber, jicama, and avocado in a medium bowl. Add salsa, oil, oregano, cumin, chili power, and a dash of cayenne. Mix well, then pour over vegetables. Add cilantro and toss gently to distribute vegetables evenly.

Salsa

³/₄ C tomatoes, chopped

¹/₄ C red bell peppers, minced

¹/₄ C yellow bell pepper, minced

¹/₄ C red onion, minced

1½ T cilantro, minced

1½ T virgin olive oil

2 t   chili powder

1   clove garlic, pressed

       dash cayenne

Combine the tomatoes, peppers, onion, and cilantro in a medium bowl. Stir in olive oil, chili powder, garlic, and cayenne.

Main Dishes

Pizza Crust

3 C   soft wheat berries, sprouted 1 day

2 C   barley, soaked 2 days

1 C   water, as needed for consistency

1   onion, chopped

1   bunch parsley, chopped

1   red bell pepper, chopped

1   tomato

4   cloves garlic

3 T   virgin olive oil

2 T   Italian seasoning

1 T   Bragg Liquid Aminos

Process all ingredients through a Champion Juicer using the solid plate. Form into a square or circular shape on a dehydrator tray with a teflex sheet. Dehydrate at 105° for 4 – 6 hours, turn crust over, and remove teflex sheet. Continue dehydrating for 8 hours or until crispy.

Pizza Paté

1 C   almonds, soaked 12 – 48 hours and blanched

1 C   pumpkin seeds, soaked 6 – 8 hours

3/4 C lentils, sprouted

1/2 C walnuts, soaked 6 – 8 hours

1/4 C sesame seeds, soaked 6 – 8 hours

1/4 C sunflower seeds, soaked 6 – 8 hours and rinsed

1 T   Bragg Liquid Aminos

1 t   paprika

1 t   kelp powder

Process nuts, seeds, and lentils through a Champion Juicer using the solid plate. Add remaining ingredients and mix well.

Pizza

Layer the following on top of the pizza crust:

- ♥ Pizza Paté

- ♥ Tomatoes, diced

- ♥ Red bell peppers, sliced

- ♥ Red onions, sliced

- ♥ Yellow squash, grated (or processed with a Cook's Help machine)

Quinoa and Adzuki Beans

1¼ C quinoa, sprouted

1 C adzuki beans, sprouted

1 C fresh corn

1 C jicama, chopped

1 C red bell peppers, chopped

¼ C fresh cilantro, chopped

2 T fresh jalapeño chili, minced

2 T red onion, minced

⅓ C lime juice

1 T virgin olive oil

½ t ground cumin

Combine all ingredients in a bowl. Spoon over lettuce leaves.

　　　　　　　　　　　Main Dishes

Spanish Rice

2 C   barley, soaked 2 days

1   medium tomato, finely chopped

¼ C   red onion, finely chopped

1 T   fresh cilantro

1 T   virgin olive oil

1 t   Bragg Liquid Aminos

1 t   Spike Salt-Free All Purpose Seasoning

½ t   ground coriander

¼ t   ground cumin

Mix all ingredients in a large bowl. If you prefer this dish warm, heat in a slightly warmed skillet no higher than 105° or place in a dehydrator at 105° for 1 – 2 hours. A great meal includes Spanish Rice, Mexican Stuffed Peppers and a green salad.

Squash Patties

2 C   sunflower seeds, soaked 6 – 8 hours and rinsed

2   carrots, finely grated

1   red bell pepper, finely chopped

1   stalk celery, finely chopped

1   yellow squash, finely chopped

1   zucchini, finely chopped

1/4 C raw tahini

2 T   flax oil

2 T   lemon juice

1 T   Bragg Liquid Aminos

      dash of cayenne

Process sunflower seeds through a Champion Juicer using the solid plate or using the "s" blade in a food processor. Add remaining ingredients and mix well. Form into round patties and refrigerate an hour before serving. Place each patty on a bed of sprouts and top with a dressing or sauce.

Main Dishes

Stuffed Peppers

4	yellow or orange bell peppers, halved and seeded
1	avocado, mashed
1	beet, shredded
1/4 C	celery, finely chopped
2 T	sunflower seeds, soaked 6 – 8 hours and rinsed
1 T	fresh parsley, chopped
1 T	lemon juice
1 t	kelp powder

Mix all the ingredients in a medium bowl, except the bell peppers. Fill pepper shells with the stuffing and top with dressing. Serve on a bed of sprouts.

Dressing:

1	avocado
1/2 – 1 C	water
2 t	Bragg Liquid Aminos
	dash cayenne

Blend all ingredients and pour over bell peppers. Save the remaining sauce for a salad dressing.

Stuffed Spinach Pesto

2 C   spinach

1/2 C   sunflower seeds, soaked 6 – 8 hours and rinsed

2   ears corn, removed from cob

1   red bell pepper, finely chopped

1   clove garlic

1 t   Bragg Liquid Aminos

In a food processor with the "s" blade, pulse chop spinach and sunflower seeds. Mix in corn, red bell pepper, garlic, and Bragg. This stuffing can be used in lettuce leaves, or stuffed in a tomato or bell pepper and served with sprouts.

Main Dishes

Tofu Tetrazzini

2 C   soybeans, soaked and sprouted

1   red onion, finely chopped

1   clove garlic, minced

2 T   tahini

2 T   virgin olive oil

2 T   fresh parsley, chopped

1 t   dried tarragon

1/2 t   dried basil

1/2 t   dried marjoram

1/4 t   cayenne

1/4 t   paprika

Process soybeans through a Champion Juicer using the solid plate or in a food processor using the "s" blade. Add remaining ingredients and mix well. Refrigerate 1 – 2 hours before serving.

Tofu
Tofu can be stuffed in cabbage leaves, lettuce leaves, spooned on top of a salad, or rolled into nori (use your imagination!)

Fiesta Tofu

2 C	soybeans, soaked and sprouted
1	carrot, finely grated
1	fennel bulb, finely diced
1	red onion, finely diced
1	tomato, finely diced
2 T	flax oil
1 T	lemon juice
2	cloves garlic, minced
1 t	chili powder
1 t	cumin

Process soybeans through a Champion Juicer using the solid plate or in a food processor using the "s" blade. Add remaining ingredients and mix well.

Main Dishes

Italian Tofu

2 C   soybeans, soaked and sprouted

½ C red onion, finely diced

1   tomato, finely diced

½ t dried basil

½ t dried oregano

½ t dried thyme

1 T Bragg Liquid Aminos

1 T lemon juice

1 T virgin olive oil

Process soybeans through a Champion Juicer using the solid plate or a food processor using the "s" blade. Add remaining ingredients and mix well.

Lemony Tofu Paté

2 C   soybean, soaked and sprouted

6   shiitake mushrooms, finely diced

2   stalks celery, finely chopped

2   shallots, minced

¼ C   vegetable juice (celery, cucumber)

2 T   fresh dill, minced

1 T   flax oil

1 t   Bragg Liquid Aminos

1 t   dried lemon peel

Process soybeans through a Champion Juicer using the solid plate or in a food processor using the "s" blade. Add remaining ingredients and mix well.

Main Dishes

Tofu Paté

2 C   soybeans, soaked and sprouted

2   stalks celery, finely sliced

1   red bell pepper, finely diced

1   red onion, finely diced

1/4 C   fresh parsley, minced

2 T   lemon juice

1 t   Bragg Liquid Aminos

1/4 t   marjoram

Process soybeans through a Champion Juicer using the solid plate or in a food processor using the "s" blade. Add remaining ingredients and mix well.

Tofu Salad Stuffed in Cabbage Leaves

2 C   soybeans, soaked and sprouted

2   stalks celery, finely sliced

1/2 C   green onions, diced

1/4 C   fresh parsley, minced

2 T   virgin olive oil

1 t   Bragg Liquid Aminos

1 t   dried orange rind

        dash cayenne

1   medium red cabbage

Process soybeans through a Champion Juicer using the solid plate or in a food processor using the "s" blade. Add remaining ingredients and mix well. Stuff into red cabbage leaves and serve on a bed of sprouts.

Tomato Fig Marinara

(Recipe by Cynthia Juenemann)

12	roma tomatoes
3/4 C	sun-dried tomatoes, soaked 5 hours (save soak water)
14	black mission figs, soaked 5 hours
6	green onions, chopped
3	cloves garlic, minced
1/2 C	fresh parsley
2 T	lemon juice
1–2 T	Bragg Liquid Aminos
1 t	oregano

Process all ingredients in a food processor using the "s" blade until smooth and blended. If the sauce needs to be thinned use the soak water from the tomatoes or figs.

Pasta:

carrot, jicama, sweet potato, yellow squash, and zucchini

Cut any combination of vegetables into julienne strips or use a Cook's Help machine to make fine spaghetti strips.

Holiday Dressing

1 C   almonds, soaked 12 – 48 hours and blanched

1 C   hazelnuts, soaked 6 – 8 hours

1 C   pumpkin seeds, soaked 6 – 8 hours

1 C   sesame seeds, soaked 6 – 8 hours

1 C   fresh parsley

1 C   white onions, finely chopped

2 T   Bragg Liquid Aminos

2 T   poultry seasoning

2 T   lemon juice

1 T   flax seeds, soaked 2 hours

½ t   kelp powder

Continued on next page

Main Dishes

Holiday Dressing
Continued

Process almonds, hazelnuts, pumpkin seeds, sesame seeds, and onions in a food processor using the "s" blade. Add remaining ingredients and process until mixture is a thick paté. Form a rounded tablespoon mixture on a dehydrator tray with a teflex sheet. Form into a 2" round or press into a well oiled, turkey – shaped cookie cutter. Remove cookie cutter and place on teflex sheet. Dehydrate at 105° for 2 hours (just until a crusty surface is formed on the outside). Turn over, remove teflex sheet, and continue dehydrating 1 – 2 hours. These should not be overdried. You want a slight moist texture wrapped around a "crisp" outside. Serve warm with your favorite sauce.

Veggie Burgers

1 C almonds, soaked 12 – 48 hours and blanched

1 C sunflower seeds, soaked 6 – 8 hours and rinsed

1 beet

1 red bell pepper

1 red onion

1 zucchini

2 carrots, finely grated

2 stalks celery, finely chopped

1/4 C fresh basil, finely chopped

1/4 C fresh parsley, finely chopped

2 T Bragg Liquid Aminos

2 T flax oil

2 T lemon juice

Process almonds, sunflower seeds, beet, red bell pepper, onion and zucchini through a Champion Juicer using the solid plate or a food processor with the "s" blade. Mix in remaining ingredients. Form into round burgers and place on a dehydrator tray with a teflex sheet. Dehydrate at 105° for 4 hours, turn burgers over and remove teflex sheet. Continue dehydrating for 4 – 6 hours, or until desired moisture is obtained. These burgers are delicious wrapped in large lettuce leaves with sprouts, tomato, and avocado.

Main Dishes

Wheat Casserole

2 C   soft wheat berries, sprouted 1 day

1 C   mung bean sprouts

½ C   red cabbage, finely shredded

4   green onions, finely chopped

2   stalks celery, finely chopped

½ C   fresh dill

2 T   lemon juice or fresh ginger juice

2 T   virgin olive oil

1 T   Bragg Liquid Aminos

        dash of cayenne

Combine all ingredients in a large bowl and serve.

Patés

Carrot Delight

5	carrots
2 C	almonds, soaked 12 – 48 hours and blanched
1 C	celery, finely chopped
¼ C	carrot juice
¼ C	green onions, finely chopped
3 T	lemon juice
1 T	Bragg Liquid Aminos
2 t	kelp powder

Process carrots and almonds through the Champion Juicer using the solid plate. Add remaining ingredients and mix well.

Patés can be used with salads, rolled in lettuce leaves, stuffed in celery, made into a burrito with large red or green cabbage leaves, or rolled in nori. I recommend using a Champion Juicer with the solid plate for the patés. The paste will be smoother; however, a food processor will also work.

Patés

"Crab" Delight

2 C   almonds, soaked 12 – 48 hours and blanched

3   stalks celery, finely chopped

1   red bell pepper, finely chopped

1/2   red onion, finely chopped

2 T   lemon juice

1 T   Bragg Liquid Aminos

1 – 2 t kelp powder

Process almonds in a Champion Juicer using the solid plate. Add remaining ingredients and mix well.

Everyone's Paté

(recipe by Don Dumont)

1 C   almonds, soaked 24 – 48 hours and blanched

½ C   sunflower seeds, soaked 6 – 8 hours

½ C   walnuts, soaked 6 – 8 hours

¼ C   pine nuts, soaked 1 hour

6   carrots

4   green onions

4   stalks celery

1   clove garlic

1   leek

½ C   sun-dried tomatoes, soaked 2 – 4 hours

2 T   Bragg Liquid Aminos

3 t   kelp powder

2 t   fresh basil or ½ t dried

2 t   fresh dill or ½ t dried

2 t   fresh oregano or ½ t dried

1   tomato, finely chopped

Process almonds, sunflower seeds, walnuts, pine nuts, carrots, green onions, celery, garlic, leek, and sun-dried tomatoes through a Champion Juicer using the solid plate or a food processor using the "s" blade. Add remaining ingredients and mix well.

Fiesta Paté

1 C   almonds, soaked 12 – 48 hours and blanched

1 C   sunflower seeds, soaked 6 – 8 hours and rinsed

1 C   lentils, sprouted

1/4 C   sesame seeds, soaked 6 – 8 hours

1   red bell pepper, finely chopped

1/2 C   celery, finely chopped

1/2 C   red onion, finely chopped

2 T   lemon juice

1 T   Bragg Liquid Aminos

2 t   chili powder

2 t   kelp powder

Process the almonds, sunflower seeds, lentils, and sesame seeds in a Champion Juicer using the solid plate or in a food processor using the "s" blade. Add remaining ingredients and mix well.

Hazelnut Paté

1½ C hazelnuts, soaked 6 – 8 hours

1½ C sunflower seeds, soaked 6 – 8 hours and rinsed

½ C sesame seeds, soaked 6 – 8 hours

1 C red bell pepper or celery, finely chopped

¾ C fresh parsley

1/2 red onion, finely chopped

2 T lemon juice

1 T Bragg Liquid Aminos

Process hazelnuts, sunflowers seeds, and sesame in a Champion Juicer with the solid plate or with a food processor using the "s" blade. Add remaining ingredients and mix well.

Patés

Mock "Tuna"

1 C   almonds, soaked 12 – 48 hours and blanched

1 C   sunflower seeds, soaked 6 – 8 hours and rinsed

¼ C   sesame seeds, soaked 6 – 8 hours

½ C   celery, chopped finely

½ C   red onion, finely chopped

½ C   fresh parsley, chopped

2 T   lemon juice

1 T   Bragg Liquid Aminos

1–2 t kelp powder

Process almonds, sunflower seeds, and sesame seeds in a Champion Juicer using the solid plate or in a food processor using the "s" blade. Add remaining ingredients and mix well.

Nut Paté

1 C   almonds, soaked 12 – 48 hours and blanched

1 C   pumpkin seeds, soaked 6 – 8 hours

1 C   sunflower seeds, soaked 6 – 8 hours and rinsed

1/4 C sesame seeds, soaked 6 – 8 hours

3   stalks celery, finely chopped

1   leek, finely chopped

1   red bell pepper, finely chopped

2 T   lemon juice

1 T   Bragg Liquid Aminos

1–2 T kelp powder

Process almonds, pumpkin seeds, sunflower seeds, and sesame seeds in a Champion Juicer using the solid plate or in a food processor using the "s" blade. Add remaining ingredients and mix well.

Patés

Pumpkin Seed Sauce

2 C   pumpkin seeds, soaked 6 – 8 hours

½ C   raisins, soaked with ¾ C water

2   bananas

½ t   nutmeg

Blend all ingredients until smooth and creamy; adjust seasonings.

South of the Border

1 C   almonds, soaked 12 – 48 hours and blanched

½ C   sesame seeds, soaked 6 – 8 hours and rinsed

½ C   sunflower seeds, soaked 6 – 8 hours and rinsed

½ C   lentils, sprouted

1   medium tomato

2   cloves garlic

½   red onion

2 T   Braggs Liquid Aminos

2 T   flax oil

1 T   mild chili powder

1 T   cumin

¼ t   cayenne

Process all ingredients in a food processor using the "s" blade until the mixture is smooth.

Patés

Spicy Hummus Dip

2 C   beans, sprouted 2 – 3 days

3   medium cloves garlic, minced

1 C   fresh parsley

1/3 C raw tahini

1/4 C minced scallions

2 T   lemon juice

1 T   Bragg Liquid Aminos

Process the garbanzo beans through Champion Juicer using the solid plate or in a food processor using the "s" blade. Add remaining ingredients and mix well.

Vegetable Paté

1 C   sunflower seeds, soaked 6 – 8 hours and rinsed

6   carrots

1   beet

1 C   spinach

2   stalks celery, finely chopped

2 T   lemon juice

1 T   Bragg Liquid Aminos

1 t   dill

Process sunflower seeds, carrots, beet, and spinach in a Champion Juicer using the solid plate or in a food processor using the "s" blade. Add celery, lemon juice, Bragg, and dill; mix well.

Patés

Salads

&

Dressings

Apple Carrot Salad

1 apple, cored and grated

2 C carrots, grated

½ C currants

½ C orange juice

2 T lemon juice

1 T lemon zest

1½ t grated fresh ginger

¼ C walnuts, soaked 6 – 8 hours, chopped

1 T shredded coconut

Combine apple, carrots, currants, orange juice, lemon juice, lemon zest, and ginger. Stir in walnuts and coconut right before serving.

Salads

Apricot Quinoa Salad

2 C	quinoa, sprouted
1/4 C	dried apricots, soaked 4 hours, finely chopped
4	green onions, finely chopped
1	red bell pepper, finely chopped
1/2 C	fresh cilantro
3 T	lemon juice
1/2 t	paprika
1/4 t	coriander
1/4 t	cumin

Combine all ingredients in a medium bowl.

Arugula Endive Salad

2	large bunches arugula, leaves only
3 – 4	heads Belgian endive
2 t	fresh parsley, minced
1 t	fresh basil, chopped
1 C	lentils, sprouted
2	cloves garlic
1 T	Bragg Liquid Aminos
1 t	dry mustard
3 T	lemon juice
½ C	virgin olive oil
1 T	lemon peel, slivered

Wash arugula well and dry on paper towels. Place leaves in salad bowl. Cut endive into quarters lengthwise about 1/4″ wide and place around the greens in bowl. Sprinkle with parsley and basil. Spoon lentils into the center. Mash garlic and mix with Bragg in a small bowl; stir in mustard and lemon juice; whisk oil. Toss salad with dressing, and add slivered lemon peel as you toss.

Salads

Asparagus Salad

1 lb	asparagus tips, cut into 2" pieces
1/4	head red leaf lettuce, torn into small pieces
1/4	head romaine lettuce, torn into small pieces
3	green onions, finely chopped
1 C	celery, thinly sliced
1/4 C	beets, finely shredded
1/4 C	flax oil
2 T	lemon juice
2 T	fresh parsley, chopped
2 t	Bragg Liquid Aminos
1 t	paprika
1/2 t	dry mustard
1/8 t	cayenne pepper

Combine asparagus, lettuce, onions, celery, and beets. In a jar, combine remaining ingredients; cover and shake well. Pour over salad and toss gently.

Asparagus 'n Guacamole

1 lb   asparagus tips, cut into 2" pieces

2   avocados, diced

2   tomatoes, sliced

1/4 C red onion, chopped

1 T   lemon juice

2 t   Bragg Liquid Aminos

2 t   virgin olive oil

1/8 t   cayenne pepper

Combine asparagus, avocado, tomatoes, and red onion. In a jar, combine remaining ingredients; cover and shake well. Pour over salad and toss gently. Serve on a bed of sprouts.

Salads

Avocado Papaya Salad

6 T   lime juice

2 – 3 dates

4 C   clover sprouts

2   large papayas, peeled, halved, pitted, then cut into quarters lengthwise

2   avocados, cut into large chunks

3   oranges, peeled and sectioned

Combine lime juice and dates in a blender. Arrange papaya quarters on four salad plates on a bed of clover sprouts. Top evenly with avocado and orange slices. Pour lime dressing over salad and serve.

Avocado Tomato Basil Salad

2	tomatoes, diced
1	avocado, diced
1 C	broccoli, cut into small pieces
1 C	cauliflower, cut into small pieces
2 T	lemon juice
2 T	virgin olive oil
2 t	Bragg Liquid Aminos
1/4 C	fresh basil, finely chopped

Combine tomatoes, avocado, broccoli, and cauliflower in a large bowl. In a jar, combine remaining ingredients; cover and shake. Pour over salad and gently toss. Serve on a bed of sprouts.

Salads

Avocado Tomato Salad

4	avocados, diced
3	tomatoes, diced
1/4 C	fresh basil
2 T	virgin olive oil
2 t	Bragg Liquid Aminos
1 t	lemon juice

Mix avocados and tomatoes in a bowl. In a jar, combine basil, olive oil, Bragg, and lemon juice; cover and shake. Pour over salad and toss gently. Serve on a bed of sprouts.

Cabbage Salad with Cumin Vinaigrette

1	medium cabbage, finely shredded
4	carrots, grated
4	green onions, finely chopped
1 C	celery, finely chopped
1/2 C	red bell peppers, finely chopped
1/3 C	flax oil
3 T	lemon juice
1 T	Bragg Liquid Aminos
1 T	whole cumin seeds
2	cloves garlic, minced

Combine cabbage, carrots, green onions, celery, and red bell pepper in a large bowl. In a jar, combine flax oil, lemon juice, Bragg, cumin seed, and garlic; cover and shake. Pour over salad and use your hands to mix well. Let marinate for 2 hours in the refrigerator before serving.

Salads

Carrot Fennel Salad

(Recipe by Karen Hedges)

6	carrots, finely sliced
6	sprigs mint
4	green onions, chopped
1	fennel bulb, finely sliced
4 T	lemon juice
2 T	flax oil
2 t	Bragg Liquid Aminos

Combine carrots, mint, green onions, and fennel in a large bowl. In a jar, combine lemon juice, flax oil, Bragg; cover and shake. Pour over salad and toss gently.

Carrots and Peas with Mint

2 C	carrots, grated
2 C	fresh peas
²/₃ C	green onions, finely chopped
¹/₂ C	fresh parsley, finely chopped
¹/₄ C	fresh mint leaves, finely chopped
¹/₂ C	virgin olive oil
2 T	lemon juice
1 t	Bragg Liquid Aminos
	fresh mint sprigs
4 C	clover sprouts or your favorite sprouts

Combine carrots, peas, green onions, parsley, and mint in a large bowl. In a jar combine olive oil, lemon, and Bragg; cover and shake. Pour over salad and toss gently. Place on a bed of clover sprouts and garnish with mint sprigs.

Salads

Carrot Salad

3 C   carrots, finely grated

½ C   raisins or currants, soaked 4 hours (discard soak water)

½ C   orange juice

¼ C   walnuts, soaked and chopped

1 T   lemon juice

1 t   zest of orange and lemon

Combine all ingredients and serve.

Cauliflower Cilantro Salad

4 C   cauliflower

1   red onion, thinly sliced and separated into rings

3 T   lemon juice

3 T   virgin olive oil

2 T   cilantro or parsley

1   clove garlic, minced

1   medium tomato, cut into wedges

Break cauliflower into florets. In a large salad bowl, combine cauliflower and onions. In a small bowl, mix lemon juice, olive oil, cilantro or parsley, and garlic; mix well. Pour dressing over cauliflower mixture, toss gently; chill for 2 hours. Before serving add tomato wedges.

Chinese Chickenless Salad

1	napa cabbage, (or some type of green cabbage) finely shredded
2 C	mung bean sprouts
1 C	snow peas, stemmed
4	green onions, finely chopped
2	stalks celery, finely chopped
1	carrot, finely grated
8	pieces of dried apricots, soaked in 1/2 C water for 4 hours (save soak water)
1/4 C	sesame seeds, soaked 6 hours
1/2 T	ginger
1/2 T	mustard
3 T	lemon juice
1/4 C	Bragg Liquid Aminos
1/4 C	flax oil

In a large bowl, layer cabbage, mung bean sprouts, snow peas, green onions, celery, and carrots. In a blender, mix remaining ingredients until smooth, using soak water to adjust consistency. Sauce should be thick but not a paste. Pour over salad and toss.

Confetti Coleslaw Salad

1 lb	cabbage, shredded
1 C	jicama, shredded
1	red bell pepper, julienned
3/4 C	carrots, shredded
1/2 C	cilantro
1	red onion, finely chopped
1	tomato
2 T	dry mustard
2 T	lemon juice
2	dates
2 t	Bragg Liquid Aminos

Combine cabbage, jicama, red bell peppers, and carrots in a large bowl. In a blender, mix cilantro, red onion, tomato, lemon juice, mustard, dates, and Bragg. Blend until smooth, pour over salad and toss gently. Chill before serving.

Salads

Corn Salad

2   ears of fresh corn

½ C   red bell peppers, chopped

¼ C   red onions, finely chopped

2 T   lemon juice

1 T   virgin olive oil

2   cloves of garlic, minced

Remove corn from cob and place in a bowl. Add remaining ingredients and mix well. Chill before serving.

Crunchy Walnut Cabbage

1 C   fresh parsley, chopped

1 C   walnuts, soaked 6 – 8 hours and chopped

1/2   medium red cabbage, shredded

1/2   medium green cabbage, shredded

1   red onion, minced

1 C   almonds, soaked 12 – 48 hours and blanched

1 C   purified water

4 T   lemon juice

1 T   Bragg Liquid Aminos

1 T   flax oil

2 t   curry powder

2 t   ginger

1 t   ground cumin

1 t   minced onion

2   cloves garlic

Combine parsley, walnuts, red cabbage, green cabbage and red onion. In a blender, add remaining ingredients and mix well. Pour dressing over salad and toss gently.

Salads

Cucumber Salad

4 C	cucumbers, thinly sliced
1	red bell pepper, cut into julienne strips
2 T	flax oil
1 T	lemon juice
1 T	fresh basil
1 T	water
1 t	Bragg Liquid Aminos
	dash cayenne
3 T	almonds, soaked 12 – 48 hours, blanched and chopped

In a mixing bowl, combine cucumber slices and red peppers; set aside. In a jar, combine flax oil, lemon juice, basil, water, Bragg, and cayenne; cover and shake well. Pour dressing over cucumber mixture, toss lightly to coat. Stir in almonds and serve.

Endive Salad with Curry Dressing

2	large heads butter lettuce
1/2 lb	Belgian endive
5 T	virgin olive oil
2 T	lemon juice
2 t	Bragg Liquid Aminos
1/2 t	dry mustard
1/4 t	curry powder
1/8 t	cardamom
1/8 t	cayenne
1	large lemon, cut into 8 thin slices

Arrange four or five butter leaves on each of four individual salad plates. Separate endive into leaves and arrange decoratively on top of lettuce. In a jar, combine olive oil, lemon juice, Bragg, mustard, curry, cardamom, and cayenne; cover and shake well. Top each salad with a lemon slice, and then drizzle with equal amounts of dressing.

Salads

Endive and Radicchio Salad

1   Belgian endive, trimmed and cut into bite-size pieces

1   bunch arugula, torn into bite-size pieces

1   head radicchio, cut into bite-size pieces

1   tomato, diced

1/4 C virgin olive oil

2 T   white onion, finely chopped

2 T   lemon juice

1 T   fresh parsley, minced

2 t   Bragg Liquid Aminos

On individual plates, arrange endive, arugula, and radicchio. In a small bowl, mix the tomato, olive oil, onion, lemon juice, parsley, and Bragg briskly with a fork. Drizzle dressing over salads.

Fiesta Bean Salad

1 C   adzuki beans, sprouted

1 C   garbanzo beans. sprouted

1 C   lentils, sprouted

1 C   mung beans, sprouted

4   stalks celery, finely chopped

2   ears fresh corn, removed from cob

2   red bell peppers, diced

1/2 C leeks, finely chopped

1/2 C lemon juice

2 T   flax oil

1 T   Bragg Liquid Aminos

1 T   cumin

1 T   chili powder

1 t   cumin seeds

2   cloves garlic, minced

Combine beans, celery, corn, red bell peppers, and leeks in a large bowl. In a small bowl, mix lemon juice, flax oil, Bragg, cumin, chili powder, cumin seeds, and garlic. Pour over beans and let marinate for at least 2 hours in the refrigerator.

Salads

Greek Quinoa Salad

2 C	quinoa, sprouted
6	red radishes, minced
4	green onions, finely chopped
1	carrot, finely grated
1	cucumber, diced
4 T	fresh parsley, minced
2 T	fresh mint
4 T	lemon juice
3 T	virgin olive oil
2 t	Bragg Liquid Aminos

Combine quinoa, radishes, green onions, carrot, cucumber, parsley, and fresh mint in a large bowl. In a small bowl or jar, mix lemon juice, olive oil, and Bragg. Pour dressing over salad and toss gently.

Green Pea Salad

2 C   green peas

1 C   sunflower sprouts

¹⁄₄ C   green onions, finely chopped

1   Fuji apple, finely chopped

1 T   mint leaves or fresh parsley, minced

Combine all ingredients in a large bowl. Toss with Garlic Tahini Dressing (page 257).

Hawaiian Salad

2	avocados, cut into large chunks
4	bananas, cut diagonally into 1″ pieces
2 T	lemon juice
2	oranges, peeled and sectioned
1	pineapple, peeled, cored, and cut into pieces
2 T	candied ginger, chopped
¼ C	flax oil
⅓ C	lime juice
2	dates
1 t	fresh ginger juice
1 t	curry powder
½ C	almonds, soaked 12 – 48 hours, blanched and chopped
	thin lime slices

Toss avocado and bananas with lemon juice; add oranges and pineapple. Sprinkle with candied ginger. In a blender, mix flax oil, lime juice, dates, ginger and curry powder. Toss fruit gently to mix, sprinkle with almonds and garnish with thin lime pieces.

Kale Salad

(Recipe by Richard Salome)

1	bunch of kale, torn into small pieces
1	red onion, finely sliced
1	avocado, diced
1 C	clover sprouts
1/3 C	lemon juice
3 T	flax oil
1 T	Bragg Liquid Aminos

Combine kale, red onion, avocado, and sprouts in a large bowl. In a small bowl, mix lemon juice, flax oil, and Bragg. Pour over salad and toss gently.

Note

This is one of my favorites. I ate this for lunch every day one summer at the beach.

Italian Bean Salad

1 C lentils, sprouted

1 C mung beans, sprouted

1/2 C adzuki beans, sprouted

1/2 C garbanzo beans, sprouted

1 C broccoli, chopped

1 C cauliflower, chopped

1 C celery, finely chopped

1 C red bell peppers, chopped

1/2 C leeks, finely chopped

3/4 C lemon juice

3/4 C virgin olive oil

1 T Bragg Liquid Aminos

1 T Italian seasoning

Combine all beans, broccoli, cauliflower, celery, red bell peppers and leeks. In a small bowl, mix lemon juice, olive oil, Bragg, and Italian seasoning. Pour over salad and toss gently. Let marinate for 1 – 2 hours in the refrigerator before serving.

Jerusalem Artichoke Salad

1 C Jerusalem artichokes, chopped

1 lb mung bean sprouts

1 C cucumber, sliced

1 tomato, sliced

3 green onions, finely chopped

1/2 C flax oil

2 T lemon juice

1 T Bragg Liquid Aminos

1 clove garlic, pressed

1/2 t dried mustard

1/4 t dried oregano

2 C mixed greens

1/2 C almonds, soaked 12 – 48 hours and blanched

Combine Jerusalem artichokes, mung bean sprouts, cucumber, tomato, and green onions in a large bowl. In a blender, mix flax oil, lemon juice, Bragg, garlic, mustard, and oregano. Pour dressing over salad and toss gently. Let marinate for 1 hour in the refrigerator. Spoon over salad greens and garnish with almonds.

Mock "Potato" Salad

2 lb	jicama, peeled and diced
1	red bell pepper, diced
1	leek, finely diced
2	stalks celery, finely diced
1	avocado, diced
4 T	fresh dill, minced or 2 T dried
1/2 C	raw tahini
1/3 C	lemon juice
1 t	cumin
1/2 t	chili powder
3 T	fresh cilantro
2	cloves garlic, pressed
2 T	Bragg Liquid Aminos

Combine jicama, red bell pepper, leek, celery, avocado, and dill in a large bowl. In a blender, mix tahini, lemon juice, cumin, chili powder, cilantro, garlic, and Bragg until creamy. Pour over salad and toss gently.

Radicchio, Red Pepper, and Avocado Salad

2	small heads radicchio (about 1/2 pound)
2	red bell peppers, cut into thin julienne strips
1	avocado, diced
4 T	virgin olive oil
2 T	lime juice
2 t	Bragg Liquid Aminos

Combine radicchio, red bell peppers, and avocado in a large bowl. In a small bowl, mix olive oil, lime juice, and Bragg. Pour over salad and toss gently.

Salads

Red Cabbage and Fennel Slaw

1	small red cabbage, finely shredded
2	stalks celery, finely chopped
5	green onions, finely chopped
1	head fennel, finely sliced
2	carrots, finely grated
6 T	lemon juice
2 T	flax oil
1 T	Bragg Liquid Aminos

Combine red cabbage, celery, green onions, fennel and carrots. In a small bowl, mix lemon juice, flax oil and Bragg. Pour over salad and toss gently.

Spanish Quinoa Salad

2 C   quinoa, sprouted

1   small red bell pepper, finely chopped

1   small yellow bell pepper, finely chopped

1 C   celery, finely chopped

4   green onions, finely chopped

1/4 C   fresh cilantro, finely chopped

2 T   fresh mint, finely chopped

2 T   lemon juice

1 T   virgin olive oil

2 t   Bragg Liquid Aminos

1/4 t   cinnamon

1/4 t   cumin

1/8 t   coriander

1/8 t   chili powder

Combine quinoa, red bell pepper, yellow bell pepper, celery, green onions, cilantro, and mint in a large bowl. In a small bowl, mix lemon juice, olive oil, Bragg, cinnamon, cumin, coriander, and chili powder. Pour over salad and toss gently.

Spinach Cauliflower Salad

1/2	large bunch spinach, torn into bite-size pieces
1/2	medium head of cauliflower, broken into florets, cut in 1/4" slices
1	large avocado, diced
6 T	flax oil
3 T	lemon juice
2 t	Bragg Liquid Aminos
1 t	dry mustard
1 t	dry basil leaves
1	large clove garlic, pressed
	dash of ground nutmeg
1/2 C	almonds, soaked 12 – 48 hours, blanched, and chopped

Combine spinach, cauliflower and avocado in a bowl. In a small bowl, mix flax oil, lemon juice, Bragg, mustard, basil, garlic, and nutmeg. Pour over salad and gently toss. Sprinkle with almonds.

Sprouted Lentil Salad

2 C   lentils, sprouted

3/4 C tomatoes, finely chopped

1/2 C clover sprouts

1/4 C green onions, minced

1/4 C fresh parsley

1/4 C celery, finely chopped

1/4 C red bell pepper, finely chopped

4 T   lemon juice

2 T   virgin olive oil

2 t   Bragg Liquid Aminos

1/4 t ground cumin

1/4 t curry powder

1 T   fresh dill, or 1 t dried

Combine lentils, tomatoes, clover sprouts, green onions, parsley, celery, and red bell peppers in a large bowl. In a small bowl, mix lemon juice, olive oil, Bragg, cumin, curry powder, and dill. Pour over salad and toss gently.

Salads

Tabouli

2 C   quinoa, sprouted

½ C   broccoli, chopped

½ C   carrots, finely grated

¼ C   red onion, finely chopped

2 T   lemon juice

1 T   flax oil

2 t   Bragg Liquid Aminos

Combine quinoa, broccoli, carrots, and red onion in a bowl. In a small bowl, mix lemon juice, flax oil, and Bragg. Pour over salad and toss gently.

Tomato Tower

½ C	yellow tomato, chopped
½ C	red tomato, chopped
1	large avocado, cut into ¼″ pieces
1 T	lime juice
½ T	fresh chives
½ T	cilantro, chopped
½ T	basil, chopped
1	medium shallot, minced
1 oz	radish sprouts or your favorite sprouts
2 t	Bragg Liquid Aminos
1 T	lemon juice
2 t	Bragg Liquid Aminos
1½ t	virgin olive oil
1½ t	flax oil

Continued on next page

Salads

Tomato Tower

Continued

Place yellow tomato in one small bowl, red tomato in another small bowl and avocado in third small bowl. Add lime juice to avocado. Sprinkle chives, cilantro, basil, and shallots evenly among the three bowls. In a small bowl, mix lemon juice, Bragg, olive oil, and flax oil. Add one fourth of the dressing to each bowl and mix gently.

Place two cylindrical molds, with their top and bottoms cut off upright on a cutting board. Pressing down firmly but gently, pack the molds with several alternating layers of red tomato, yellow tomato and avocado. Finish with a final layer of avocado. Carefully slide a spatula between the cutting board and cylinder bottom. Lift the cylinder onto chilled plates and carefully remove the mold leaving "towers" on plate. Garnish with sprouts and drizzle a little dressing around the plates.

Avocado Dill Dressing

1	avocado
1	cucumber, cut into chunks
2 T	virgin olive oil
1 T	lime juice
2 t	Bragg Liquid Aminos
2 t	dried dill

In a blender, mix all ingredients until smooth and creamy; adjust seasonings to taste.

Avocado Tomatillo Dressing

1	avocado
2	tomatillos
1/2	cucumber
1 T	Bragg Liquid Aminos
1/4 t	dried dill
1/8 t	chili powder

In a blender, mix all ingredients until smooth and creamy; adjust seasonings to taste.

Avocado Tomato Dressing

1	avocado
1 t	tomato
1/2	cucumber
2 T	flax oil
1 T	lemon juice
1 t	basil
1 t	oregano
1 t	thyme

In a blender, mix all ingredients until smooth and creamy; adjust seasonings to taste.

Carrot Celery Dressing

1 C   carrots, shredded

2   stalks celery, chopped

1/2   cucumber

1/4 C almonds, soaked 12 – 48 hours and blanched

2 t   Bragg Liquid Aminos

In a blender, mix all ingredients until smooth and creamy; adjust seasonings to taste.

Carrot Dressing

1	avocado
1 C	carrot juice
1/4 C	celery juice
1 T	Bragg Liquid Aminos
1 t	ginger
1 t	lemon

In a blender, mix all ingredients until smooth and creamy; adjust seasonings to taste.

Cilantro Dressing

¾ C celery juice

¾ C fresh cilantro, finely chopped

¼ C lemon juice

3 T   raw tahini

2 T   flax oil

1   clove garlic, minced

       dash cayenne

In a blender, mix all ingredients until smooth and creamy; adjust seasonings to taste.

Creamy Garlic Dressing

½ C   sunflower seeds, soaked 6 – 8 hours and rinsed

½ C   flax oil

¼ C   lemon juice

1   clove garlic, pressed

1 t   dry mustard

In a blender, mix all ingredients until smooth and creamy; adjust seasonings to taste.

Cucumber Dill Dressing

1   cucumber

3 T   flax oil

2 T   lemon juice

2 T   virgin olive oil

2 T   fresh dill or 2 t dried

1 T   Bragg Liquid Aminos

¼ t   dry mustard

In a blender, mix all ingredients until smooth and creamy; adjust seasonings to taste.

Cucumber Dressing

1	cucumber
1	green onion, chopped
3	honey dates
¼ C	lemon juice
¼ C	water
1 t	fresh dill weed
1	clove garlic, minced (optional)

In a blender, mix all ingredients until smooth and creamy; adjust seasonings to taste.

Curry Dressing

²/₃ C virgin olive oil

¹/₂ C lemon juice

4   honey dates

1¹/₂ T curry powder

In a blender, mix all ingredients until smooth and creamy; adjust seasonings to taste.

Garlic and Herb Dressing

¼ C   lemon juice

2   cloves garlic, pressed

½ C   flax oil

½ C   virgin olive oil

1 t   Bragg Liquid Aminos

½ t   paprika

¼ t   dried basil

¼ t   dried mint

¼ t   dried oregano

¼ t   dried thyme

In a bowl, mix garlic with lemon juice. Gradually add the flax oil
and olive oil, whisking all the time so that the dressing
homogenizes. Stir in herbs.

Garlic Mustard Dressing

1¼ C   virgin olive oil

¾ C   lemon juice

3 – 4 T dry mustard

1 t   Bragg Liquid Aminos

        dash of cayenne

6   cloves garlic, pressed

In a blender, mix lemon juice, mustard, Bragg, cayenne, and garlic.
Slowly add olive oil in a steady stream and blend.

Garlic Tahini Dressing

1/4 C flax oil

2 T lemon juice

2 T water

1½ T raw tahini

2 t Bragg Liquid Aminos

1/2 t dried chervil

1/2 t dried oregano

1 clove garlic

In a blender, mix all ingredients until smooth and creamy; adjust seasonings to taste.

Goddess Dressing

1	avocado
1	red bell pepper
2	green onions, chopped
3 T	lemon juice
1/2 – 1 C	water
1 T	Bragg Liquid Aminos
1 t	cumin
	dash of cayenne

In a blender, mix all ingredients until smooth and creamy; adjust seasonings to taste.

Herbal Salad Dressing

½ C	lemon juice
¼ C	flax oil
¼ C	virgin olive oil
1 T	Bragg Liquid Aminos
1	clove garlic, minced
2 t	dry mustard
½ t	dried basil
½ t	dried chervil
½ t	dried savory
¼ t	ground coriander
¼ t	dried oregano
¼ t	dried thyme
⅛ t	dried sage

In a blender, mix all ingredients until smooth and creamy; adjust seasonings to taste.

Dressings

Italian Basil Dressing

2	tomatoes
2 C	fresh basil, firmly packed
½ C	almonds, soaked 12 – 48 hours and blanched
2 T	virgin olive oil
1 T	Bragg Liquid Aminos
1	clove garlic, minced
	water for consistency

In a blender, mix all ingredients until smooth and creamy; adjust seasonings to taste.

Italian Sunflower Dressing

1 C   sunflower seeds, soaked 6 – 8 hours and rinsed

1/4 C flax oil

1/4 C lemon juice

1 T   Bragg Liquid Aminos

1/2 t dried basil

1/2 t dried oregano

1/2 t dried thyme

In a blender, mix all ingredients until smooth and creamy; adjust seasonings to taste.

Lemon Dressing

½ C   flax oil

6 T   lemon juice

1 T   fresh chives

1 T   fresh dill

1 T   fresh thyme, or 1 t dried

1 t   Bragg Liquid Aminos

In a blender, mix all ingredients until smooth and creamy; adjust seasonings to taste.

Lemon Parsley Dressing

4 T   lemon juice

2 T   flax oil

1 T   lemon zest

1/2 C parsley, finely chopped

1 T   red pepper, finely chopped

In a blender, mix all ingredients until smooth and creamy; adjust seasonings to taste.

Dressings

Lemon Tarragon Dressing

½ C lemon juice

¼ C flax oil

1 T   fresh tarragon, finely chopped

1 t   dry mustard

⅛ t   cayenne

In a blender, mix all ingredients until smooth and creamy; adjust seasonings to taste.

Mint Dressing

¼ C   sunflower seeds, soaked 6 – 8 hours and rinsed

½   yellow onion

¾ C   water

½ C   fresh mint

⅓ C   lemon juice

1 T   raw tahini

2 t   Bragg Liquid Aminos

2   cloves garlic, minced

In a blender, mix all ingredients until smooth and creamy; adjust seasonings to taste.

Orange Dressing

1 C   orange juice

3 T   raw tahini

3   dates

2   cloves garlic, minced

1 T   lemon juice

In a blender, mix all ingredients until smooth and creamy; adjust seasonings to taste.

Sesame Dill Dressing

¼ C   sesame seeds, soaked 6 hours

¼ C   orange juice

1 T   fresh dill or 1 t dried

1 T   flax oil

1 T   lemon juice

2 t   Bragg Liquid Aminos

In a blender, mix all ingredients until smooth and creamy; adjust seasonings to taste.

Spicy Cucumber Dressing

½ C   sunflower seeds, soaked 6 – 8 hours and rinsed

½ C   cucumber, chopped

1 T   raw tahini

2 t   lemon juice

2   cloves garlic, minced

         dash cayenne

In a blender, mix all ingredients until smooth and creamy; adjust seasonings to taste.

Thousand Island Dressing

2	red bell peppers
2	tomatoes
1 C	celery, chopped
½ C	pine nuts, soaked 2 hours
½ C	sunflower seeds, soaked 6 – 8 hours and rinsed
½ C	fresh parsley
½–1 C	water
4 T	lemon juice
2 T	Bragg Liquid Aminos

In a blender, mix all ingredients until smooth and creamy; adjust seasonings to taste.

Dressings

Tomato Herb Dressing

1	tomato
¼ C	virgin olive oil
1½ T	fresh tarragon, or ½ t dried
1 T	fresh basil, or 1 t dried
1 T	lemon juice
2 t	Bragg Liquid Aminos
	dash of cayenne

In a blender, mix all ingredients until smooth and creamy; adjust seasonings to taste.

Tomato Salad Dressing

1 C   tomato juice

1/4 C flax oil

1/4 C virgin olive oil

3 T   lemon juice

1 T   fresh basil, finely chopped

1/4 t   dried oregano

1   clove garlic, minced

In a blender, mix all ingredients until smooth and creamy; adjust seasonings to taste.

Tomato Tahini

1½ C   tomato juice

¼   yellow onion

2 T   raw tahini

1 T   lemon juice

2   cloves garlic, minced

In a blender, mix all ingredients until smooth and creamy; adjust seasonings to taste.

Smoothies

Apple Pear Smoothie

2   apples

2   pears

1   banana

Blend ingredients and serve.

Apricot Pineapple Smoothie

6   apricots

2   bananas

1/4 C   pineapple

Blend ingredients and serve.

Banana Kiwi Smoothie

3   bananas

2   kiwis

1   orange

Blend ingredients and serve.

Berry Peach Smoothie

2   apples

2   peaches

1/2 C   blackberries

1/2 C   raspberries

Blend ingredients and serve.

Blackberry Fruit Smoothie

1 C   blackberries

2   apples

2   bananas

Blend ingredients and serve.

Blueberry Smoothie

1 C   blueberries

3   bananas

Blend ingredients and serve.

Cactus Pear
Breakfast Smoothie

2	cactus pears, peeled and chunked
1	banana
1 C	almond milk
6	honey dates

Blend ingredients and serve.

Cherry Banana Smoothie

1 C	dried bing cherries, soaked 3 hours
2	bananas

Blend ingredients and serve.

Fresh Fruit Smoothie

1 C	strawberries
2	apples
2	oranges

Blend ingredients and serve.

Smoothies

Green Juice

3	kiwis
2	bananas
1	apple
1	orange
1	papaya
2 C	sunflower sprouts
1/4 C	spirulina powder

Blend ingredients and serve. This juice is very healing.

Orange Banana Smoothie

2	oranges
2	bananas

Blend ingredients and serve.

Peach Smoothie

2	peaches
2	pears
2	plums
1/2 C	blackberries

Blend ingredients and serve.

Persimmon Smoothie

6   persimmons

2   bananas

Blend ingredients and serve.

Persimmon Apricot Smoothie

2   persimmons

4   dried black mission figs, soaked

2   dried apricots, soaked

Blend ingredients and serve.

Pineapple Cranberry Smoothie

1 C   fresh pineapple

1/4 C fresh cranberries

5   dates

1   frozen banana

Blend ingredients and serve.

Pineapple Date Smoothie

1 C   fresh pineapple

5   dates

1   frozen banana

Blend ingredients and serve.

Pineapple Strawberry Smoothie

1 C   fresh pineapple

1 C   frozen strawberries

Blend ingredients and serve.

Strawberry Smoothie

1 C   strawberries

½ C   boysenberries

2   apples

2   bananas

Blend ingredients and serve.

Strawberry Banana Smoothie

1 C   strawberries

3   bananas

Blend ingredients and serve.

Super Guava Boost

2   apples

2   oranges

1   guava

1 C   red flame grapes

½ C   strawberries

Blend ingredients and serve.

Super Juice

1 C   red flame grapes

1 C   strawberries

2   apples

2   oranges

1   guava

Blend ingredients and serve.

Smoothies

Tropical Delight

3   bananas

1   mango

1 C pineapple

Blend ingredients and serve.

Soups

Avocado Cauliflower Cream

2 C. cauliflower, chopped

1 C   water

¹/₄ C almonds, soaked 12 – 48 hours and blanched

1   avocado

2 t   Bragg Liquid Aminos

In a blender, mix all ingredients. Garnish soup with chopped almonds.

Optional:
Add your favorite seasoning such as cayenne, chili, cumin, curry, or basil.

Soups can be warmed to 105° and will still be full of enzymes. Be sure to use a thermometer and a very low heat. Also, you can use vegetables at room temperature.

Broccoli Soup

2 C   broccoli

2 C   sprouts (sunflower, buckwheat, peat shoots, clover
       or any combination)

1 C   celery juice

3   dates

1 T   flax oil

2 t   Bragg Liquid Aminos

1 t   dry mustard

In a blender, mix all ingredients and serve.

Butternut Squash Soup

2 C   butternut squash, diced

³/₄ C barley, soaked 2 days

¹/₂ C dates

1   avocado

1 t   nutmeg

      water

In a blender mix all ingredients. Add enough water to make a thick souplike consistency.

Cabbage Soup Swedish Style

4 C   cabbage

2 C   sprouts (sunflower, buckwheat, pea shoots, clover or any combination)

1 C   fresh tomato juice

1 C   fresh vegetable juice (celery, cucumber, parsley)

1   onion

1 T   flax oil

2 t   caraway seeds

In a blender, mix all ingredients and serve.

Cabbage Soup with a Zest

4 C   cabbage

2 C   sprouts (sunflower, buckwheat, pea shoots, clover
         or any combination)

1 C   fresh vegetable juice (combination of celery, cucumber,
         tomato)

1   red bell pepper

1   onion

1 T   virgin olive oil

2 t   caraway seeds

1/2 t   dried basil

1/2 t   dried savory

1/2 t   dried thyme

In a blender, mix all ingredients and serve.

Cabbage Sweet and Sour Soup

4 C   cabbage

2 C   sprouts (sunflower, buckwheat, pea shoots, clover or any combination)

1 C   vegetable juice (celery, cucumber, tomato)

2   carrots, finely grated

1   red bell pepper

1   onion

2   carrots, chopped

4   medjool dates

1 T   flax oil

2 t   Bragg Liquid Aminos

In a blender, mix all ingredients and serve.

Cabbage Tomato Soup

1 C   fresh tomato juice

4 C   cabbage

2 C   sprouts (sunflower, buckwheat, pea shoots, clover
       or any combination)

1 C   fresh tomato juice

3   red bell peppers

1/2   small yellow onion

1 T   virgin olive oil

1   clove garlic

In a blender, mix all ingredients and serve.

Carrot Curry Soup

5	carrots, chopped
2 C	sprouts (sunflower, buckwheat, pea shoots, clover or any combination)
1 C	vegetable juice (celery, cumber, tomato)
1	onion
1 T	lemon juice
1 T	virgin olive oil
2 t	Bragg Liquid Aminos
1/2 t	cumin
1/2 t	curry

In a blender, mix all ingredients and serve.

Carrot Dill Soup

5   carrots, chopped

2 C   sprouts (sunflower, buckwheat, pea shoots, clover or any combination)

1 C   vegetable juice (celery, cucumber)

1   onion

½ C   fresh dill

2 T   flax oil

2 t   Bragg Liquid Aminos

In a blender, mix all ingredients and serve.

Carrot Sunflower Soup

4   carrots, grated

2 C   sprouts (sunflower, buckwheat, pea shoots, clover or any combination)

1 C   fresh vegetable juice (celery, cumber, tomato)

½ C   orange juice

¾ C   sunflower seeds, soaked 6 – 8 hours and rinsed

2 t   Bragg Liquid Aminos

In a blender, mix all ingredients and serve.

Curried Squash Soup

2	butternut squash
2 C	sprouts (sunflower, buckwheat, pea shoots, clover or any combination)
1 C	orange juice
1-2 C	water
1/2 C	chopped yellow onion
3/4 t	ground ginger
1/2 t	cinnamon
1/2 T	cumin
1/2 t	coriander
1/4 t	dry mustard
1	clove garlic
	dash of cayenne
1/4 C	almonds, soaked 12 – 48 hours and blanched

In a blender, mix all ingredients. Garnish soup with chopped almonds and serve.

Cauliflower Soup

1	cauliflower
2 C	sprouts (sunflower, buckwheat, pea shoots, clover or any combination)
1 C	fresh vegetable juice (celery, cucumber, tomato)
4	carrots, chopped
1	yellow onion
1 T	lemon juice
1 T	virgin olive oil
½ t	cumin
½ t	dry mustard
½ t	ginger
½ t	turmeric
1	clove garlic, minced
	dash of cinnamon
	dash of cayenne pepper

In a blender, mix all ingredients and serve.

Corn Chowder

2   ears corn, removed from cob

2   parsnips, chopped

2 C   jicama, chopped

1   stalk celery, chopped

1-1½ C water

¼ C   almonds, soaked 12 – 48 hours and blanched

1   ear corn, removed from cob, set aside

¼ C   red bell pepper, finely chopped

In a blender, mix 2 ears of corn, parsnips, jicama, and celery. Add water for consistency. Stir in 1 ear of corn kernels. Garnish with almonds and red pepper.

Soups

Cucumber Dill Soup

2 C   celery, chopped

2 C   sprouts (sunflower, buckwheat, pea shoots, clover
       or any combination)

1 C   cucumber juice

6   green onions, chopped

2 T   fresh dill

1 t   lemon juice

2 t   Bragg Liquid Aminos

In a blender, mix all ingredients and serve.

Lentil Bolognese

1 C	brown or green lentils, sprouted
1 C	cucumber juice
2 C	tomatoes
1	carrot, chopped
1	stalk celery
1¼ C	onion
2 T	virgin olive oil
1 t	dried oregano
2	cloves garlic, pressed
2 t	Bragg Liquid Aminos

In a blender, mix all ingredients and serve.

Pumpkin Soup

1½ C fresh pumpkin, chopped

1 C fresh vegetable stock (juice 4 – 5 stalks celery and
      ½ cucumber

1   red bell pepper

½   avocado

½   red onion

½ C almonds, soaked 12 – 48 hours and blanched

1 T   virgin olive oil

1   clove garlic, minced

¼ t   chili powder

In a blender, mix all ingredients and serve.

Red Pepper Fennel Soup

2	red bell peppers
2 C	sprouts (sunflower, buckwheat, pea shoots, clover or any combination)
1 C	fresh vegetable juice (celery, cucumber, tomato)
1	fennel bulb
1	yellow onion
1 T	virgin olive oil
2	cloves garlic, minced
1 t	curry powder
1 t	fennel seeds
2 t	Bragg Liquid Aminos

In a blender, mix all ingredients and serve.

Soups

Spicy Squash Soup

4   zucchini, chopped (or your favorite squash)

2 C   sprouts (sunflower, buckwheat, pea shoots, clover or any combination)

1 C   vegetable juice (celery, cucumber, tomato)

2   Anaheim peppers

1   carrot, chopped

1   yellow onion

½ C   cilantro

1 T   virgin olive oil

2   cloves garlic, minced

2 t   cumin

1 T   Bragg Liquid Aminos

In a blender, mix ingredients and serve.

Squash Dill Soup

5	medium summer squash (or your favorite squash)
2 C	sprouts (sunflower, buckwheat, pea shoots, clover or any combination)
1 C	vegetable juice (celery and cucumber)
1	yellow onion
1	bunch fresh dill
1 T	virgin olive oil
2 t	Bragg Liquid Aminos

In a blender, mix all ingredients and serve.

Soups

Spicy Tomato Soup

5	tomatoes
4	honey dates
2 C	sprouts (sunflower, buckwheat, pea shoots, clover, or any combination)
1½ C	yellow onions, chopped
1 T	virgin olive oil
1 T	fresh dill weed
¼ C	parsley, chopped
3	cloves garlic, pressed

In a blender, mix all ingredients. Garnish soup with parsley.

Squash Soup

5	summer squash (or your favorite squash)
2 C	sprouts (sunflower, buckwheat, pea shoots, clover or any combination)
1 C	vegetable juice (celery, cucumber, carrot, tomato)
1 T	flax oil
1/4 t	nutmeg
5	green onions, chopped

In a blender, mix squash, sprouts, vegetable juice, flax oil, and nutmeg until smooth. Garnish soup with green onions and serve.

Tomato Carrot Soup

5	very ripe tomatoes
4	carrots, chopped
2 C	sprouts (sunflower, buckwheat, pea shoots, clover or any combination)
1 C	vegetable juice (celery and cucumber)
1 T	virgin olive oil
2 t	Bragg Liquid Aminos
1 t	tarragon
2	leeks, chopped

In a blender, mix tomatoes, carrots, sprouts, vegetable juice, olive oil, Bragg, and tarragon until smooth. Garnish with chopped leek and serve.

Tomato Pesto Soup

6	very ripe tomatoes
2 C	sprouts (sunflower, buckwheat, pea shoots, clover or any combination)
1 C	vegetable juice (celery and cucumber)
1	yellow onion, chopped
1 C	fresh basil
1 T	virgin olive oil
2 t	Bragg Liquid Aminos
1/4 t	oregano
3	cloves garlic, minced

In a blender, mix all ingredients and serve.

Yam Apple Soup

2	small yams
1	apple, cored and chopped
2 C	sprouts (sunflower, buckwheat, pea shoots, clover or any combination)
1 C	apple juice
1 C	vegetable juice (celery and cucumber)
4	shallots
1 T	flax oil
2 t	Bragg Liquid Aminos
1 t	lemon juice
1/4 t	cardamom
1/4 t	nutmeg

In a blender, mix all ingredients and serve.

Zucchini Soup

4   zucchini

2 C   sprouts (sunflower, buckwheat, pea shoots, clover or any combination)

1 C   tomato juice

2 t   Bragg Liquid Aminos

1 t   virgin olive oil

1/8 t   marjoram

1/8 t   thyme

In a blender, mix all ingredients and serve.

Zucchini Soup Italian Style

6	tomatoes
3	zucchini
1	carrot, chopped
1	yellow onion, chopped
2 C	sprouts (sunflower, buckwheat, pea shoots, clover or any combination)
2 T	virgin olive oil
1 T	fresh oregano
1 T	fresh basil
2 t	Bragg Liquid Aminos
3	cloves garlic, minced

In a blender, mix all ingredients and serve.

Recommended Reading

Conscious Eating, Gabriel Cousens, MD, Essene Vision Books

Spiritual Nutrition and the Rainbow Diet, Gabriel Cousens, MD, Cassandra Press

Biogenic Living The Essene Way, E. B. Szekely, International Biogenic Society

Dining in the Raw, Rita Romano, Kensington Publishing

Enzyme Nutrition, Edward Howell, Avery Publishing

Fasting Can Save Your Life, Herbert Shelton, American Natural Hygiene Society

Intuitive Eating, Humbart Sontillo, Hohm Press

Juice Fasting and Detoxification, Steve Meyerowitz, The Sprout House

Living Foods for Optimum Health, Brian R Clement with Theresa Foy DiGeronimo, Prima Publishing

Nature's First Law: The Raw-Food Diet, Stephen Arlin, Fouad Dini, David Wolfe, Maui Brothers Printing

Perfect Body, Roe Gallo, ProMotion Publishing

Sprout It!, Steve Meyerowitz, The Sprout House

Super Nutrition, Herbert Shelton, Willow Publishing

Super Nutrition Gardening, Peavy and Peary, Avery Publishing

Recommended Reading

Survival into the 21st Century, Victoras Kulvinskas, MS, Century Publishing

The Lover's Diet, Victor P. Kulvinskas, MS, Ramesh Lahiri, 21st Century Publications, Inc. and L.O.V.E. Foods Inc.

The Sprouting Book, Ann Wigmore, Avery Publishing Group Inc.

The Wheatgrass Book, Ann Wigmore, Avery Publishing Group Inc.

Your Health...Your Choice, M. Ted Morter, DC, Morter Health System

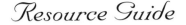

Resource Guide

Barlean's Organic Oils
4936 Lake Terrell Road
Ferndale, WA 98248
www.barleans.com
1-(800) 445-3529 toll free

Flaxseed oil is the world's richest source of Omega-3 fatty acids. Omega-3s have been extensively researched for their preventative and therapeutic properties in over 60 diseases and illness. While beneficial, Omega-3s are susceptible to degradation from heat, light and oxygen. Barlean's is the only company to manufacture, ship and distribute Fresh ExPressed™ flaxseed oil, ensuring consumers of the freshest and most nutritious flaxseed oils. To locate a health food store near you that sells Barlean's Fresh ExPressed™ Oils, call the toll-free number.

Date People
P. O. Box 808
Niland, CA 92257
(760) 359-3211

The Date People carry over 50 varieties of organic dates and their specialty is soft dates. The dates are raw, fresh and non-hydrated. They have great prices, fast services, and quality dates.

Diamond Organics
P. O. Box 2159
Freedom, CA 95019
1-(888) 674-2642 toll free
Fax: 1-(888) 888-6777

Jasch and Kathleen Hamilton

Diamond Organics offers year-round shipping of organic produce, including wheatgrass, many types of sprouts, fruits, vegetables, greens, herbs, flowers, and roots. No minimum order and direct home delivery.

Resource Guide

The Sprout House
17267 Sundance Drive
Ramona, CA 92065
1-(800) 777-6887 toll free
Fax: (760) 788-7979

The Sprout House carries many varieties of organic sprouting seeds and growing kits for indoor sprouting without soil, and they ship fresh wheatgrass. Also, they carry how-to books on sprouting.

The Sproutpeople
225 Main Street
Gays Mills, WI 54631
1-(877) 777-6887 toll free
(608) 735-4735
Fax: (608) 735-4736

The Sproutpeople carry a wide selection of organic seeds and sprouting supplies.

Sundance Country Farm
P.O. Box 2429
Valley Center, CA 92082
1-(888) 269-9888 toll free
Fax: (760) 751-1141

Stan Fink

Sundance carries an extensive line of dried fruits, dehydrated vegetables, dates, maple sugar and syrup, date sugar, oils, raw almond butter, raw tahini, carob, bee pollen, herbs, spices, teas, and more.

Sunflower Farms
12033 Woodinville Drive #22
Bothell, WA 98011
(425) 488-5652

Sunflower Farms ships buckwheat lettuce, sunflower greens, wheatgrass and pea greens, all certified organic by the state of Washington. They also have a mix that is available seasonally.

Index

A

Almond Cookies 108
Almond Orange Cookies 109
Apple Carrot Salad 209
Apple Muffins 63
Apple Pear Smoothie 273
Apple Pie 138
Apple Raisin Cookies 110
Apple Strawberry 153
Apple Walnut Pie 139
Apricot Almond Bread 53
Apricot Cookies 111
Apricot Muffins 64
Apricot Pineapple Smoothie 273
Apricot Quinoa Salad 210
Apricot Truffles 101
Arise and Shine 153
Arugula Endive Salad 211
Asparagus 'n Guacamole 213
Asparagus Salad 212
Avocado Cauliflower Cream 281
Avocado Dill Dressing 245
Avocado Dulse Dip 35
Avocado Papaya Salad 214
Avocado Tomatillo Dressing 246
Avocado Tomato Basil Salad 215
Avocado Tomato Dressing 247
Avocado Tomato Salad 216

B

Banana Bread 54
Banana Cookies 112
Banana Ice Cream 128
Banana Kiwi Smoothie 273
Banana Muffins 65
Banana Nut Cookies 113
Banana Nut Cream Torte 85-86
Banana Persimmon Ice Cream 128
Basil Pesto 36
Bean Dip 37
Berry Peach Smoothie 274
Berry Pie 140
Blackberry Fruit Smoothie 274
Blueberry Ice Cream 129
Blueberry Muffins 66
Blueberry Smoothie 274
Breakfast Muffins 67
Brendan's High Energy Bars 114
Broccoli Soup 282
Butternut Squash Soup 283

C

Cabbage Salad 217
Cabbage Soup Swedish Style 284
Cabbage Sweet and Sour Soup 286
Cabbage Tomato Soup 287
Cabbage Soup With a Zest 285

Cactus Pear Breakfast Smoothie 275
Carob Fudge Sauce 136
Carob Ice Cream 129
Carob Mint Cookies 115
Carob Mint Ice Cream 130
Carrot Cake 87-88
Carrot Celery Dressing 248
Carrot Cookies 116
Carrot Curry Soup 288
Carrot Delight 197
Carrot Dill Soup 289
Carrot Dressing 249
Carrot Fennel Salad 218
Carrot Hummus 161
Carrot Raisin Bread 55
Carrot Raisin Muffins 68
Carrot Salad 220
Carrot Salsa 38
Carrot Sunflower Soup 290
Carrots and Peas with Mint 219
Cauliflower Cilantro Salad 221
Cauliflower Soup 292
Cherry Banana Smoothie 275
Chili 162
Chinese Chickenless Salad 222
Chunky Apple Cookies 117
Cilantro Barley 163
Cilantro Dressing 250
Cinnamon Date Bread 56
Citrus Shine 153

Living in the Raw

Living in the Raw

Order Form

FOR ADDITIONAL COPIES OF THIS BOOK, PLEASE CALL

Telephone: 1-(877) 557-4711 (orders only)
Fax: 1-(831) 421-9280
E–mail: roselee@rawlivingfoods.com

Mail orders:

Rose Publishing

P. O. Box 2274

Santa Cruz, CA 94063

Please send me _____ copies of *Living in the Raw*

Name:_____

Address:_____

City:_____

State:_____ Zip:_____

Price: $17.95 + $2.00 postage & handling

Priority mail, add $3   Overnight mail, add $15

Payment: Check _____   Money order _____

Thank you for your order!

Order Form

FOR ADDITIONAL COPIES OF THIS BOOK, PLEASE CALL

Telephone: 1-(877) 557-4711 (orders only)
Fax: 1-(831) 421-9280
E–mail: roselee@rawlivingfoods.com

Mail orders:

Rose Publishing

P. O. Box 2274

Santa Cruz, CA 94063

Please send me _____ copies of *Living in the Raw*

Name:_____

Address:_____

City:_____

State:_____ Zip:_____

Price: $17.95 + $2.00 postage & handling

Priority mail, add $3   Overnight mail, add $15

Payment: Check _____   Money order _____

Thank you for your order!

My Free Gift to You

An audio tape on how to maintain a raw living food lifestyle. (Value $9.95)

Fill out form and send $1.00 for postage to:

Rose Lee Calabro
P O Box 2274
Santa Cruz, CA 95063

Name _____

Address_____

City_____

State, Zip_____

Phone No._____